Collected rhymes, stories, songs and information text

Me & my home

Author
Rebecca Taylor

Editor
Jane Bishop

Designers
Heather Sanneh and Lynda Murray

Compilers
Stories, rhymes and information text compiled by Jackie Andrews
Songs compiled by Peter Morrell

Assistant Editors
Lesley Sudlow and Saveria Mezzana

Series Designer
Anna Oliwa

Illustrations
Terry Burton

Cover artwork
Alex Ayliffe

Acknowledgement:
Qualifications and Curriculum Authority for the use of extracts from the QCA/DfEE document *Curriculum guidance for the foundation stage* © 2000 Qualifications and Curriculum Authority.

The publishers gratefully acknowledge permission to reproduce the following copyright material:

Jackie Andrews for 'My rabbit' © 2001 Jackie Andrews, previously unpublished; **Barbara Ball** for 'Porridge and pictures' © 2001 Barbara Ball, previously unpublished; **Clive Barnwell** for 'My house' © 2001 Clive Barnwell, previously unpublished; **Clive and Hannah Barnwell** for 'Paint my face' © 2001 Clive and Hannah Barnwell, previously unpublished; **Ann Bryant** for 'Paul and the great big freezer', 'A new home for a mole?' and 'Out in my back garden' © Ann Bryant 2001, all previously unpublished; **Susan Eames** for 'My jobs' © 2001 Susan Eames, previously unpublished; **John Foster** for 'Today's my birthday' from *Whizz Bang Orang Utan* © 1999 John Foster (1999, OUP); **John Foster** for 'Skip down the path' from *Bare Bear and Other Rhymes* © 1999 John Foster (1999, OUP); **John Foster** for 'The morning rush' © 2001 John Foster, previously unpublished; **Trevor Harvey** for 'Missing' © 2001 Trevor Harvey, previously unpublished; **Karen King** for 'Tessa's new home', 'That pup!', 'Delivering the food' and 'Going shopping by the sea' © 2001 Karen King, all previously unpublished; **Patricia Leighton** for 'Leroy in a mood' © 2001 Patricia Leighton, previously unpublished; **Johanne Levy** for 'Growing', 'A pet to call my own' and 'Celebration!' © 2001 Johanne Levy, all previously unpublished; **Wes Magee** for 'In my toy-box I have got...' and 'Who likes grapefruit?' © 2001 Wes Magee, both previously unpublished; **Tony Mitton** for 'Washday', 'My bed', 'Listening in bed' and 'Guess who?' © 2001 Tony Mitton, all previously unpublished; **Peter Morrell** for 'That's my chair!' © 2001 Peter Morrell, previously unpublished; **Judith Nicholls** for 'Me!' © 2001 Judith Nicholls, previously unpublished; **Sue Nicholls** for 'Which face today?' © 2001 Sue Nicholls, previously unpublished; **Clare West** for 'Looking after ourselves' © 2001 Clare West, previously unpublished; **David Whitehead** for 'Sounds lovely' © 2001 David Whitehead, previously unpublished; **Stevie Ann Wilde** for 'Splishy splashy!', 'New shoes' and 'A favourite place' © 2001 Stevie Ann Wilde, all previously unpublished; **Brenda Williams** for 'I have a baby sister' and 'My house' © 2001 Brenda Williams, both previously unpublished.

Every effort has been made to trace copyright holders and the publishers apologize for any inadvertent omissions.

Text © 2001 Rebecca Taylor
© 2001 Scholastic Ltd

Designed using Adobe Pagemaker

Published by Scholastic Ltd, Villiers House, Clarendon Avenue, Leamington Spa, Warwickshire CV32 5PR
Visit our website at www.scholastic.co.uk

1234567890   1234567890

British Library Cataloguing-in-Publication Data A catalogue record for this book is available from the British Library.

ISBN 0 439 01727 0

The right of Rebecca Taylor to be identified as the author of this work has been asserted by her in accordance with the Copyright, Designs and Patents Act 1988.

All rights reserved. This book is sold subject to the condition that it shall not, by way of trade or otherwise, be lent, hired out or otherwise circulated without the publisher's prior consent in any form of binding or cover other than that in which it is published and without a similar condition, including this condition, being imposed upon the subsequent purchaser.

No part of this publication may be reproduced, stored in a retrieval system, or transmitted, in any form or by any means, electronic, mechanical, photocopying, recording or otherwise, without the prior permission of the publisher. This book remains copyright, although permission is granted to copy pages where indicated for classroom distribution and use only in the school which has purchased the book and in accordance with the CLA licensing agreement. Photocopying permission is given only for purchasers and not for borrowers of books from any lending service.

Contents

Introduction
Wishing Well: Me and my home **5**

Rhymes
Skip down the path **6**
Guess who? **8**
My house **10**
Me! **12**
Sounds lovely **14**
My bed **16**
Listening in bed **18**
I have a baby sister **20**
Washday **22**
In my toy-box I have got… **24**
Missing **26**
Today's my birthday **28**
The morning rush **30**
Splishy, splashy! **32**
Who likes grapefruit? **34**

Stories
Tessa's new home **36**
A new home for a mole? **38**
Leroy in a mood **40**
Paul and the great big freezer **42**
Porridge and pictures **44**
That pup! **46**

Information text
A favourite place **48**
New shoes **50**
My rabbit **52**
Delivering the food **54**
Going shopping by the sea **56**

Songs
My house **58**
That's my chair! **60**
My jobs **62**
Out in my back garden **64**
Growing **66**
Looking after ourselves **68**
Paint my face **70**
Which face today? **72**
A pet to call my own **74**
Celebration! **76**

Early years wishing well: Me and my home

Contents

Photocopiables

Animal sounds **78**
Alphabet washing line **79**
Colourful bear **80**
Food, glorious food **81**
Pussy cat, pussy cat **82**
Lift-the-flap freezer **83**
Word bingo dice **84**
Word bingo board **85**
Shape pictures **86**
Puppet show **87**
Patterned tie **88**
Blast off! **89**
My special day **90**
Glasses and flowers **91**
Flower power **92**
Toothbrush design **93**
Cats' legs **94**
Dot to dot **95**
The flap house **96**

Early years wishing well: Me and my home

Introduction

Wishing Well: Me and my home

The *Wishing Well* series is designed to help early years practitioners by providing a selection of rhymes, stories, songs and information text all linked to a popular theme. The ideas for using these resources are all written to support the Early Learning Goals (QCA) across all six areas of learning.

Theme

'Me and my home' is an important topic for young children as it is where their earliest experiences will be taking place. They will feel confident and happy talking about their own homes and the things that happen there. They will also be able to physically explore their own homes to answer any questions that you may ask of them.

Using an anthology

The resources provided in this book will enable you to use rhymes, stories, songs and information text, written at the correct level, to introduce the curriculum to early years children. All the photocopiable material is new and will save hours of planning time.

It is important at this age to stimulate the children by providing experiences with all writing genre. In particular, poems will appeal to young children, who have short concentration spans, because they are able to quickly engage with the text and learn from the ideas provided.

Early Learning Goals

Each idea for using the material is directly linked to the requirements of the Early Learning Goals, covering all six areas – Personal, social and emotional development; Communication, language and literacy; Mathematical development; Knowledge and understanding of the world; Physical development and Creative development.

Using this book

The book is divided into sections, one for each type of resource, with rhymes, stories, songs and information texts all stored in separate chapters. Each rhyme, story, song or piece of information text is presented opposite a page of easy-to-refer-to activity ideas. The activity ideas are all bullet-pointed so that they can be quickly referred to in planning meetings. You can either plan to work through each activity in turn, or take an activity from each section so that the children receive a variety of rhymes, stories, songs and information text each week.

Either way, you will be certain to provide your children with a broad, balanced and stimulating curriculum.

The photocopiable sheets, on pages 78 to 94, are referred to within the text, so that it is quite clear where they link with the main activities. Pages 95 and 96 are more general and can be used to support any work carried out on this topic.

Rhymes

Skip down the path

Skip down the path.
Hide in the shed.
Race round the roses.
Stand on your head.

Roll in the grass.
Swing on the swing.
Jump in the air.
Dive through the ring.

Slide down the slide.
Chase round the tree.
Run out of breath.
Go in for tea!

© John Foster

photocopiable

Early years wishing well: Me and my home

Rhymes

Skip down the path

Personal, social and emotional development
★ Talk to the children about how they feel after physical exercise. Explain that it is sometimes good to feel out of breath and this means that they have been working their heart and muscles very hard.
★ After physical activity sessions, always have a quiet time when the children can sit on cushions and listen to soft music to relax before their next activity.

Communication, language and literacy
★ Read the poem to the children very fast, and then very slowly, and see if they can join in each time.
★ Ask the children to think about their own gardens and have a picture of them in their minds. Be very sympathetic to each child's circumstances. If some of the children do not have a garden, encourage them to think of perhaps a relative's or friend's garden or a visit to a park. Write some rules on a flip chart about what you should do in a garden such as not walk on the flower beds.

Mathematical development
★ Organize an outing to your local park and introduce a maths theme. Tell all your helpers that you would like the children to count houses and trees as they walk to the park and see if they can spot two- and three-dimensional shapes in the buildings they pass.

★ Ask the children to go home and find out how many paces it takes for them to reach their front door from their gate. Do they have a long path or a short path? Ask them to find out how many paces it takes for one of their parents to do the same route.

Knowledge and understanding of the world
★ In your setting, provide a nature table that reflects the season. In the autumn, it could have pine-cones and leaves; in the spring, it could have a vase of flowers, and in the summer, it could have special shells and a tub of sand to touch.

Physical development
★ In a large open space, encourage the children to skip independently bringing their knees up each time.
★ Progress on to skipping with hoops and then ropes. If you have a very large rope, two adults could hold it a little way above the ground and each child could take a turn at running towards it and jumping.

Creative development
★ Help the children to make a handprinted tree to display next to the nature table. Use green and orange paint, and talcum powder to make a snowy tree.
★ Make rose prints using sponges cut to shape. Print bright colours for the petals and add stems using a paintbrush.

Early years wishing well: Me and my home

Rhymes

Guess who?

Can you guess?
Are you sure?
Who's this coming
to your door?

Rustle, rustle.
What's that?
A letter landing
on the mat.
Who can that be?

Rattle, rattle.
Clink, clink.
Two fresh bottles
of milk to drink.
Who can that be?

On the path –
sound of shoes.
Through the letter box:
Daily News.
Who can that be?

Did you guess
(were you sure?)
who it was
at your front door?

© Tony Mitton

photocopiable

Early years wishing well: Me and my home

Rhymes

Guess who?

Personal, social and emotional development
★ Ensure that you always have high security at your setting and that the children know that they must never open the front door – that is always the responsibility of an adult.
★ Set up a house in your home corner, with, if possible, a three-sided screen that has a door. Provide the children with props to help them re-enact visitors coming to the door, for example, envelopes for a postperson, plastic bottles for a milk deliverer and a newspaper for the person delivering the papers.

Communication, language and literacy
★ As you read the poem to the children, write down the people who they think are being described. Draw a picture of the visitor next to the name to help the children recognize the word. Encourage the children to think of other visitors that come to their homes and add these to the list.
★ Ask each child to bring in an envelope with their home address on and a stamp. Help the children to each draw a picture and write a short letter to their parents. Organize a walk to the local post-box to post the letters.
★ Choose one child to stand in front of you with his or her back to the rest of the group. Ask him or her to make a telephone noise. Choose another child (from the rest of the group) to answer by saying 'hello'. The child being a telephone then has to guess, without turning around, who in the group has answered the phone.

Mathematical development
★ Ask the children to find out their house number and write it down on a class list.

Knowledge and understanding of the world
★ Invite people who visit your nursery on a regular basis, such as postal workers, refuse collectors and milk deliverers, to talk to the children about their work and the number of houses that they have to visit each day.

Physical development
★ Sit the children in a circle and choose one child to start. This child should walk around the circle while everyone sings, *'I sent a letter to my love and on the way I dropped it, someone must have picked it up and put it in their pocket. Please, please, drop it, drop it. Please, please, drop, drop it.'* The child who is walking drops a letter behind someone's back. This child then has to chase the leader back to their place.

Creative development
★ Use plastic milk bottles filled with rice and pasta to create percussion instruments. Decorate with wrapping paper. Vary the amount of pasta and/or rice in each bottle and encourage the children to identify the differences in the sounds.

Early years wishing well: Me and my home

Rhymes

My house

(Action rhyme)

My house is so tall
(stand on tiptoe reaching up)

My house has a wall
(spread arms and legs wide)

My house has a door
(pretend to open a door and walk through)

My house has a floor
(stamp on ground)

My house has a tree
(arms waving above head)

My house has me!
(point to self)

© Brenda Williams

photocopiable

Early years wishing well: Me and my home

Rhymes

My house

Personal, social and emotional development

★ Ask each child to bring in a photograph of their house and display them with labels such as, 'This is Robert's house'.

★ Give the children some construction equipment and encourage them to make houses for their soft toys. Provide them with a large sheet of paper to build their houses on and then invite them to draw roads and roundabouts between the houses.

Communication, language and literacy

★ Draw a big picture of a house on a flip chart and encourage the children to help you label it using their initial sound knowledge.

★ Create a sound tray and put a variety of objects that begin with 'h' onto it, such as hats and toy houses.

★ Provide the children with an outline of a house and encourage them to write the letter 'h' all over it to practise their handwriting.

Mathematical development

★ Give the children a variety of objects that are tall and short and encourage them to sort them into two hoops.

★ Encourage the children to draw objects that are wide, such as a motorway.

★ Make a graph of all the different types of houses that the children live in, such as terraced, semi-detached, detached house, flat or bungalow.

Knowledge and understanding of the world

★ If you can, ask a builder to come to your setting and build a very small wall. Encourage the children to observe how the bricks tessellate together and how they are not just piled on top of each other. Let the children try some brick laying, using construction bricks to make house models.

★ Ask the children to think about how we clean up our homes and how recycling our rubbish is a really good idea.

★ Introduce a mini-recycling station in your setting to help encourage the children to clean up. Provide a newspaper box, a can box and an aluminium foil box and invite the children to use them.

Physical development

★ As you read the rhyme to the children, encourage them to carry out the actions as described. Change the pace of your voice and invite them to do their actions slowly and then quickly. Next, ask them to work in pairs and to do the actions together as you read the rhyme.

Creative development

★ Ask the children to take some rubbings in their homes using paper and wax crayons. Invite them to look for unusual textures. They may find textured wallpaper or bathroom tiles. Show them how to lay the paper flat and carefully rub over the surface.

Early years wishing well: Me and my home

Rhymes

Me!

Becky likes to fly a kite,
Ben to dance and sing;
Joel always chooses paints,
Florence loves to swing.

Hannah's good at football,
Paul climbs every tree;
Zachary loves biking,
A book is good for *me*.

Rosie's always dreaming,
Izzy's full of smiles;
Christy is a chatterbox,
Josh can run for *miles*.

Francis has a pinkish skin
And short straight hair, like Lee;
Billy's curly, brown and tall
But I...

Only I am *ME!*

© Judith Nicholls

photocopiable

Early years wishing well: Me and my home

Rhymes

Me!

Personal, social and emotional development
★ Celebrate each child's individual successes with regular 'showing' times when they can show any awards, such as swimming or dance certificates, that they have achieved and talk about what they like to do in their spare time.
★ Have a table where children can place any special objects that they have brought from home so that other children can look at them.

Communication, language and literacy
★ Say to the children, 'Listen carefully, I am going to describe someone in the room and I would like you to try to guess who it is'. Describe a child by their characteristics and by how they look. Remember to remain sensitive to individual children.
★ Play 'I spy' with the children building on their initial sound knowledge.
★ Create a book with each child drawing a picture of what they like to do. Write a sentence underneath describing what is in the picture, for example, 'Claire likes to do ballet'.

Mathematical development
★ Set the children a practical problem. If they invited four friends to tea, how many chairs would they need at the table in total? Remind them not to forget themselves when thinking about this.
★ If everyone took their shoes off, how many individual shoes would there be?

★ As you read the rhyme to the children, encourage them to count how many different children are described.
★ Create a tally chart of the things that the children like to do and then count up to find out which is the most popular activity.

Knowledge and understanding of the world
★ Ask the children to think about what they enjoyed doing yesterday in their house and what they would like to do tomorrow. Encourage them to use the appropriate vocabulary to describe their past and future.

Physical development
★ Ask the children to show, in actions, what they like to do. For example, if they like swimming, they could lie on the floor and kick their legs madly. If they like flying a kite, they could pretend to stand holding a string. Encourage the children to watch each other and guess what they are doing.

Creative development
★ Ask the children to paint a picture of themselves, paying great attention to the colours that they use. Take the opportunity to develop their initial sound knowledge by labelling each paint pot with the initial sound of the colour inside.
★ Invite the children to role-play some of the activities mentioned in the rhyme. Can the others guess what they are doing?

Early years wishing well: Me and my home

Rhymes

Sounds lovely

I love –
The sound of fish and chips
Frizzling in the fat.

I love –
The sound of purring
From our plump, contented cat.

I love –
The sound of seaside shingle
Tumbled in the tide.

I love –
The sound of wind and rain
When I am snug inside.

But best of all –
The sound I love
Is the clinking and the clank
As I drop my pocket money
In my china piggy bank.

© David Whitehead

Early years wishing well: Me and my home

Rhymes

Sounds lovely

Personal, social and emotional development
★ Create a 'letter-of-the-alphabet shop', for example, the 'b' shop, with everything in the shop beginning with the letter 'b' such as ball, bear and bat.
★ Set up a hardware shop where you can buy items to use in the home such as dusters, brushes and buckets.
★ In both shops, give the children the opportunity to use real money.

Communication, language and literacy
★ Encourage the children to sit quietly for one minute. Invite them to listen to the sounds that they can hear in your setting. Ask them to help you make a list of all the sounds heard, such as footsteps, someone breathing, someone talking.
★ Set up a cassette recorder in a quiet corner and ask each child to go and speak into it, for example, 'My name is Ben and my favourite sound is sausages sizzling in the pan'.

Mathematical development
★ Ask the children if they have a piggy bank and if they like hearing the sound of money going into it. Show them some real coins and let them handle them, take rubbings of them and draw around them.
★ Give older children a pot of pennies to count. Encourage them to put them into piles of ten, then five and two.

Knowledge and understanding of the world
★ Provide large yoghurt pots and a ball of string to make string telephones. Ensure that the children keep the string really taut so that the telephones work properly.
★ Go on a sound walk around your local area, encouraging the children to stop occasionally and listen to sounds such as birds singing, milk bottles being clanged together and the sound of the wind.
★ Give each child a copy of the photocopiable sheet on page 78 and encourage them to write in the sounds that the animals make and then link each animal with the correct home.

Physical development
★ Play the game 'What's the time, Mr Wolf?'. You play the wolf at one end of the room and the children stand at the other. The children have to tiptoe quietly when the wolf's back is turned. They say 'What's the time, Mr Wolf?', and you say a time, for example, '6 o'clock' – they must take six steps towards you. When you shout 'dinner time', the children must run wildly as you try to catch them.

Creative development
★ Set up a screen with some musical instruments behind it and play each instrument one by one. Encourage the children to listen carefully and predict which instrument you are playing.

15

Early years wishing well: Me and my home

Rhymes

My bed

My bed is like a little boat
floating out to sea.
And now it's like an island
with a coconut tree.

My bed is like a racing car
roaring in a race.
And now it's like a rocket
rising into space.

My bed is like a submarine
diving down deep.
And now my bed is just a bed
because I'm fast asleep.

© Tony Mitton

16
photocopiable

Early years wishing well: Me and my home

My bed

Personal, social and emotional development
★ Create a 'yellow submarine' in your role-play area. Staple thick cardboard onto the outside of your screen and paint it yellow. Make a control panel for the inside of the submarine and provide card and writing materials so that the children can send postcards home.
★ During circle time, invite each child to say why they like their bed and what colour their duvet cover is.

Communication, language and literacy
★ Encourage the children to help you finish the sentence 'My bed is like a…' with their own ideas. Write their sentences on a flip chart showing how you put your finger spaces in between words and how you carefully form your letters.

Mathematical development
★ Provide each child with an outline of a car and ask them to decorate it. Then, number each car and hang them up in your setting so that the children can refer to them as a number line.
★ Draw out a race track, with five lanes, on a large piece of card. Make a start and a finish. Ask the children to race the cars on the track and use mathematical vocabulary such as, 'Look, the red car came first and the green car came second'.

Knowledge and understanding of the world
★ In your water play area, give the children a variety of objects to test to see if they float or sink. Include a sponge to show the children how it floats at first but then starts to sink as it absorbs water.
★ Using a square of balsa wood, a lolly stick and a triangle of white paper, help the children to make a boat. Take it to your water play area and encourage the children to find different ways of getting it across the water. Can they blow it, flick it and push it?
★ Invite the children to think about how their bed is covered. Show them a variety of materials and ask them, 'If you needed to make a bed for an animal, which materials would you use?'.

Physical development
★ During the summer months, organize some fun races such as a dressing-up race where the children have to put on a hat and some wellington boots and run a short distance.

Creative development
★ Teach the children the words of the song, 'We All Live in a Yellow Submarine' by The Beatles found in *Abracadabra Guitar!* by Hilary Bell (A & C Black) and encourage them to sing it while playing in your role-play area.
★ Invite the children to make a papier mâché island from newspaper and card, and to decorate it with paint.

Early years wishing well: Me and my home

Rhymes

Listening in bed

If I listen hard
in bed at night,

I can hear
the floor creak,
the door squeak,
the tap leak.

I can hear
the dishes clink
down in the kitchen sink.

I can hear the telly boom
down in the sitting room.

And very near
I can hear
my little brother
breathing deep.
Sssssh...
He's fast asleep.

© Tony Mitton

Listening in bed

Personal, social and emotional development
★ Encourage the children to share experiences of their little brothers and sisters. What do they like doing with them? Be sensitive to any children who do not have brothers or sisters.

Communication, language and literacy
★ Make an audio cassette of noises that occur in the home such as the sounds of the vacuum cleaner and doorbell. Ask the children to listen very carefully to identify them.
★ Occasionally, during story time, tell the story with a puppet. This will really excite the children and motivate them as well as developing their listening skills.
★ Timetable a regular television session for the children. Tape-record an educational programme you would like them to watch if it is not broadcast at a convenient time.

Mathematical development
★ Write the rhyme on a flip chart and encourage the children to count how many letters are in each word. Make a list of two-letter words and three-letter words.

Knowledge and understanding of the world
★ Encourage the children to think about machines that they hear at night in their homes such as a washing machine, a dishwasher or a fridge. Ask them to think about other machines that do the work for us around the home. If they could invent a new machine, what would it do?
★ After carrying out cookery activities together, always take a bowl of warm soapy water to the table so that the children can help with the washing-up.
★ Encourage the children to identify their favourite sounds in their houses. How do the sounds make them feel? Could they share their favourite sounds, using their voices and body percussion?

Physical development
★ Play a game of 'sleeping lions' after any energetic game. The children lie down and pretend to go to sleep and you walk around and see if any 'lion' is moving.

Creative development
★ Help the children to make a bed for their teddies using cereal boxes for the mattress and tubes for the legs. Ask them to bring in their bears so that they can select the right-sized box for them. Provide squares of material for bedding.
★ Sit the children into a circle and put a variety of musical instruments in the middle. Ask one child to stand in front of you with their back to the rest of the children. Invite another child to tiptoe into the middle and play an instrument. The child standing up will have to guess which instrument is being played.

Early years wishing well: Me and my home

Rhymes

I have a baby sister

I have a baby sister
Who is very very new
Her face is pink and wrinkly
And I think her eyes are blue.

I peeped at little sister
As she lay in my old cot
She's really rather tiny
And doesn't say a lot.

I offered her my finger
She waved and held on tight
I have a brand new sister
Who only came last night.

© Brenda Williams

Early years wishing well: Me and my home

Rhymes

I have a baby sister

Personal, social and emotional development

★ If you know of a mother with a new baby, invite her into your setting so that the children can observe how the baby behaves. Encourage the children to keep very quiet when the mother and baby come in and tell them that babies do not like loud or sudden noises. Ask the mother to talk to the children about how she cares for her baby and allow the children to draw on their personal experiences.

★ Provide a cot and bedding for a pretend baby in the home corner so that the children can role-play looking after it.

Communication, language and literacy

★ Encourage the children to help you write a letter to the baby who is described in the rhyme. Encourage them to think about how to start a letter and how to end it. What could they say to the baby?

★ Invite the children to help you make a list of words that describe babies such as sweet, cuddly and tiny.

Mathematical development

★ Count how many children have blue or brown eyes. Which is the most popular eye colour in the group?

★ Can the children count their fingers and their toes and tell you how many they have got altogether?

Knowledge and understanding of the world

★ Show the children a variety of pictures of animals and ask the children to name their babies. For example, a cow has a calf and a horse has a foal.

★ Create an interactive table of old and new objects so that the children can learn important vocabulary to help them to describe the past and the future.

★ Ask the children to help you make a list of things that they can do but that a baby cannot. Some of the comparisons they may think of could be: a baby drinks from a bottle but they use a cup, and a baby sleeps in a cot but they sleep in a bed.

Physical development

★ Provide the children with mats in a large open area and encourage them to do rolls. Teach them how to do a log roll by lying straight with their arms stretched out. Then show them how to do an egg roll by pulling their knees up to their chest and rolling.

Creative development

★ Talk to the children about toys that babies enjoy and help them to make a mobile for a baby. Provide a cardboard ring and help them to draw pictures on a piece of card that they think a baby might like. Tie the pictures onto the ring. Encourage the children to draw pictures on both sides of the card because the ring will twirl around.

Early years wishing well: Me and my home

Rhymes

Washday

(Rhythmic action poem)

I'm pushing the clothes
in the washing machine.
      *(mime pushing the clothes
      into the front of the machine)*
They're dirty now
but they'll come out clean.

The clothes go round
and round and round,
      *(make circles in the air with hands
      to show washing going round)*
with suds and bubbles
and a swishing sound.

I'm hanging the clothes up
one by one.
They'll dry in the breeze
and the hot, bright sun.

Lift and peg
and lift and peg,
    (lift and peg in rhythm to the words)
sleeve of shirt
and trouser leg.

When they're dry
they're a tangly mess,
so I get out the iron
and give them a press.

Fold and press
and fold and press.
      *(fold with one hand, press
      iron along with the other)*
wrinkly shirt
and creased-up dress.

Now it's the end
of washing-day,
so I pile up the clothes
and put them away.

Pile and pat
and pile and pat.
Close up the cupboard
That's that!
    *(mime piling and patting in rhythm, then close
    cupboard door, then brush hands together in
    gesture of finality in time to last two beats)*

© Tony Mitton

Early years wishing well: Me and my home

Rhymes

Washday

Personal, social and emotional development
★ Create a launderette in your role-play area using large cardboard boxes, painted white with a round door cut out of the front. Provide plastic washing baskets, clothes and empty soap boxes and fabric conditioner plastic bottles.
★ Encourage the children to discuss how they help their parents to do the washing. Do they help with the folding or holding the pegs?

Communication, language and literacy
★ Create a washing line in your setting by making outlines of clothes such as socks, vests and T-shirts on bright pieces of card. Write a letter of the alphabet with a thick black pen on each piece of card. Peg the cardboard outlines onto a washing line strung up across your setting, for the children to refer to. Give each child a copy of the photocopiable sheet on page 79 and encourage the children to practise correct letter formation.

Mathematical development
★ Encourage the children to count the number of outlines on your washing line.
★ On a large piece of card, draw a washing line with ten items on it and number them from one to ten. With two children, two counters and a dice, help them to see who can be the first to get to the end of the washing line.

Knowledge and understanding of the world
★ Have regular 'wash days' in your setting. Fill your water tray with warm and soapy water and invite the children to wash all of the toy's clothes.
★ Ask the children to find out where they wash their clothes at home. Have they ever visited a launderette?
★ Talk to the children about irons. What do they know about them? (Hopefully, they will say that they are very hot and that you must never touch them!) Encourage the children to think of other appliances in the home that are very hot and that they should never touch, such as the oven and the toaster.

Physical development
★ Ask the children to act out the rhyme as you say it to them, miming all the actions with exaggerated movements.
★ Provide the children with large table-cloths and encourage them to work as a group to fold them in half and then into quarters.

Creative development
★ Give the children regular opportunities to do free painting, encouraging them to paint whatever they choose. Hang the paintings up on washing lines in your setting to dry. Ask the children what they would like to call their painting, then write down their title and their own name and display the captions next to the paintings.

Early years wishing well: Me and my home

Rhymes

In my toy-box I have got...

...a red balloon,
a quacking duck,
a rocking horse,
a sit-on truck...

...two dinosaurs,
a model farm,
a teddy bear,
with just one arm...

...a ball, a bike,
Old Captain Hook,
Spotty Snake,
and this new book...

© Wes Magee

In my toy-box I have got...

Personal, social and emotional development
★ Ask each child to bring in their favourite toy and talk about it to the group. Encourage them to tell others why their toy is special, who gave it to them and where it is kept in their home.

Communication, language and literacy
★ Have a colour table in your setting to show objects of a particular colour. Include a sign saying the name of the colour. Change the chosen colour regularly.
★ Stimulate the children with colour by providing them with coloured play dough, coloured water in the water tray and encouraging them to wear a particular colour of clothes on a specific day.
★ Encourage each of the children to draw a picture of their favourite toy and stick the pictures into a scrapbook. Help the children to draw doors, cupboards, plants or dustbins to make flaps over the toys in the book. Stick the flaps on and then write sentences in the book such as, 'Can you find our toys hiding in this cupboard?'.

Mathematical development
★ When you are working alongside the children using the model farm, ask mathematical questions such as, 'How many chicks are there?', 'How many sheep are there?', 'Can you put the horses into pairs?'.
★ Sit the children in a circle and place a large quantity of toys in the middle. Next to the toys, place two hoops. Ask one child to put three teddy bears in one hoop and another child to place two dolls in the other. Have a third child count all the toys by touching them one by one. Repeat with different amounts of toys and different children.

Knowledge and understanding of the world
★ Invite the children to ask their parents what their favourite toy was when they were little and why.
★ Create a display of toy dinosaurs and small information books about dinosaurs. Encourage the children to think about why we do not have dinosaurs today.

Physical development
★ Give the children opportunities to ride your sit-on trucks and vehicles in the outdoor play area. Make it more exciting by chalking out a 'road' and providing a zebra crossing for pedestrians. Add some soft-toy hazards along the way for the children to avoid.

Creative development
★ Provide the children with a large outline of a paper balloon and encourage them to paint a bright pattern on it. When they have finished, ask them to staple a strip of crêpe paper onto the top edge and hang them up in your setting.

Early years wishing well: Me and my home

Missing

Has anyone seen a furry old bear?
I've hunted here
And I've hunted there,
I've looked up high
And I've looked down low –
Under the bedclothes
Where he likes to go,
Inside the cupboard
Where he likes to hide,
In the back of the car
Where he likes to ride –
So, has anyone seen a furry old bear?
I still can't find him –
ANYWHERE!

© Trevor Harvey

Early years wishing well: Me and my home

Missing

Personal, social and emotional development

★ In your role-play area, use a large box or lots of little boxes to create a car that the children can pretend to go on adventures in. Provide props such as a car rug, a map and a picnic basket to use when they arrive at their destination.

Communication, language and literacy

★ Talk to the children about the importance of posters and how they can tell lots of people a message, such as that you have lost something. Encourage the children to help you design a poster to tell everyone that the bear is lost. Remind them that not many words are used on a poster so it may just say in big letters 'Missing bear'.

★ Give each child a copy of the photocopiable sheet on page 80. Help them to select the right colours for each part of the bear and then encourage them to complete it.

★ Write the rhyme on a flip chart. Have some cards to write on. Ask the children to think about how you could change some words in the rhyme and substitute their own onto the cards. For example, instead of the line 'under the bed clothes', the children may decide 'under the rug'.

Mathematical development

★ Help the children to weigh toy cars or, if you have them, plastic teddies in large bucket scales. Encourage them to find out if they can make the scales balance. Use language such as 'heavier' and 'lighter'.

★ Ask the children to make a repeating pattern with the cars and plastic teddies. For example, they might place a car on the floor, then a teddy next to it, then a car, then a teddy. Encourage them to make other repeating patterns with objects that they find in your setting.

Knowledge and understanding of the world

★ Create a materials table where the children can go and handle different materials and describe them. Encourage vocabulary such as 'this is furry' and 'this is smooth'.

★ Talk to the children about where they like to go in their parents' cars. What do they do when they are in the car? Do they count how many red cars they see?

Physical development

★ In your outdoor area, show a small group of children how to play hide-and-seek. Play inside too, by hiding a toy before the children arrive and then setting them the challenge of finding it. Provide them with clues by saying 'warm', 'cold', 'very cold', 'hot'.

Creative development

★ Give the children some strips of card and encourage them to make hats and scarves for their own teddies.

Early years wishing well: Me and my home

Today's my birthday

Today's my birthday.
Now I'm four.
I'm one year older
Than I was before.

I measured myself
Against the wall
And I'm over a hundred
Centimetres tall –

Much taller than
I used to be,
When I was small
And only three.

Today's my birthday.
Now I'm four.
I'm older and bigger
Than I was before.

© John Foster

Rhymes

Today's my birthday

Personal, social and emotional development

★ Display a chart that reads, 'Today is a special day for…'. Encourage each child to stick their name onto the sign with Blu-Tack when it is their birthday.
★ During circle time, give each child the opportunity to say what they do on their birthday and what they like to give other people when it is their birthday.
★ Give the children a badge to wear on their special day so that the other children know that it is their birthday.

Communication, language and literacy

★ Ask the children to make a birthday card for someone special. Talk about what should be written inside a birthday card.
★ Collect story-books that are about someone celebrating their birthday and display them in your book corner with a sign saying 'All these books are about birthdays'.
★ Invite the children to think about which room in their house is the best place to have a party in. Encourage them to share experiences of parties that they have had in their own home.

Mathematical development

★ Invite the children to help you to arrange a small group of them into height order from the smallest to the tallest. Talk about what they have found out. Who is the tallest? Are there any children in the group who are the same size?
★ Ask the children to lie on a very large piece of paper and draw around them. Encourage the children to use different materials to measure their outline and ask, 'How many cars/teddy bears do you measure?'.

Knowledge and understanding of the world

★ Tie a long piece of string across your room to represent a timeline. Encourage the children to bring in pictures of themselves as babies, and baby clothes to peg up at one end. At the other end, peg up photographs of the children now, along with clothes that they wear, so that the children can see how they have changed over time.
★ Use the computer to make birthday cards for a child in your group. Let the children type in a message and use clip art to decorate it.

Physical development

★ Encourage the children to move on the apparatus, firstly in a very tall way and then in a very small way, using different body parts. Ask the children to watch each other and decide whether they are being tall or small.

Creative development

★ Talk about how we are entertained at parties. Organize a mini talent show with each child having the opportunity to sing, dance or tell a joke to the rest of the group.

Early years wishing well: Me and my home

The morning rush

Into the bathroom,
Turn on the tap.
Wash away the sleepiness –
Splish! Splosh! Splash!

Into the bedroom,
Pull on your vest.
Quickly! Quickly!
Get yourself dressed.

Down to the kitchen.
No time to lose.
Gobble up your breakfast.
Put on your shoes.

Back to the bathroom.
Squeeze out the paste.
Brush, brush, brush your teeth.
No time to waste.

Look in the mirror.
Comb your hair.
Hurry, scurry, hurry, scurry
Down the stairs.

Pick your school bag
Up off the floor.
Grab your coat
And out through the door.

© John Foster

The morning rush

Personal, social and emotional development

★ Ask your local dentist to visit your setting and talk to the children about how important it is to clean their teeth regularly, and to visit the dentist to have them checked.

★ Using a piece of card, create a big shoe and thread a thick lace through it. Invite the children to go to it regularly and practise learning how to tie their shoelaces.

★ Create a shoe shop in your role-play area that has lots of different types of shoes, shoeboxes, carrier bags and rulers.

Communication, language and literacy

★ Let the children design a poster encouraging other children to clean their teeth. Remind the children that posters do not usually have many words and it may just say 'Remember to clean your teeth'.

★ Invite the children to help you write a list of ways in which getting ready in the morning could be less of a rush. These could include laying their clothes out, making their lunch and laying the breakfast table the night before.

Mathematical development

★ Show the children how to make a clock with moveable hands using a paper plate, card for the hands, a paper fastener and twelve small paper circles, that the children can write individual numbers on. Demonstrate to the children how to stick the number 12 at the top of the plate, 6 at the bottom and then the 3 half-way between the 12 and the 6, and the 9 opposite it. Show how the other numbers then fit in. Allow them to decorate the middle of their clock.

★ Give the children a piece of paper and divide it into four squares. Ask them to draw four things that they have to do in the morning, making sure that they are in the right order.

Knowledge and understanding of the world

★ Provide the children with a selection of magazines and encourage them to make a collage of foods that are healthy and not healthy to eat for breakfast.

★ Invite the children to think of all the technology which they use at home each morning. This might include an alarm clock, a radio, a television or a microwave.

Physical development

★ Encourage the children to role-play activities that they do in the mornings using big movements.

Creative development

★ Provide the children with catalogues and a paper outline of a house, divided into four rooms. Encourage the children to cut out pictures of furniture, sort them and stick them into the correct room.

Early years wishing well: Me and my home

Rhymes

Splishy, splashy!

My mum is always painting things
In the kitchen and the hall.
She chooses colours I don't like,
That I'd never choose at all.

I like blue and green and red
And yellow and pink and white.
So she's painted my room like a rainbow,
All splishy and splashy and bright.

© Stevie Ann Wilde

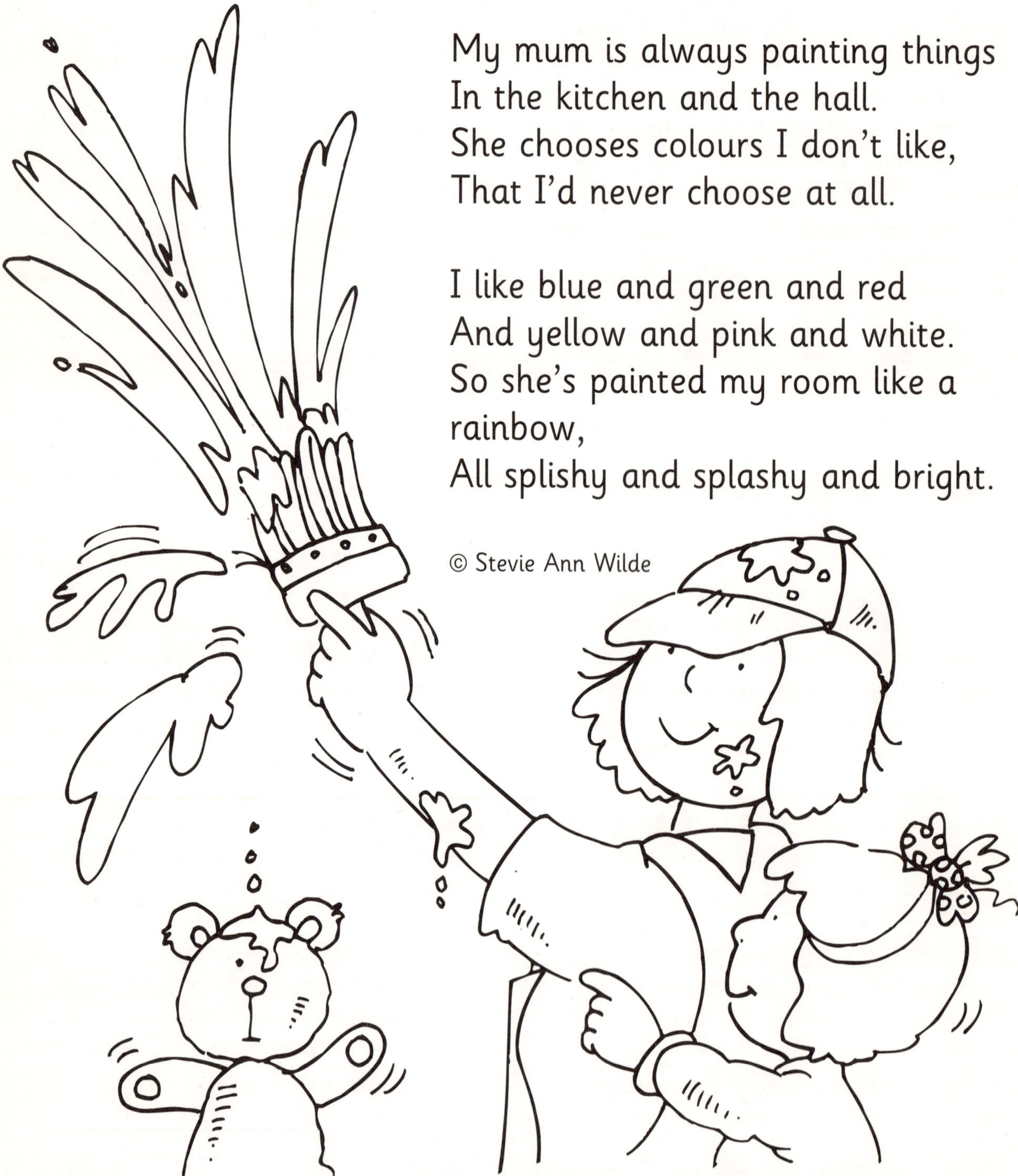

Early years wishing well: Me and my home

Rhymes

Splishy, splashy!

Personal, social and emotional development
★ Show the children a variety of coloured cards. Encourage them to think about how different colours make them feel. Which colours make them feel happy? Which colours make them feel sad? For example, how does the colour red make them feel? What does red mean on a traffic light? What does it mean when you go to the seaside and see a red flag flying?

Communication, language and literacy
★ Ask the children to find out what colour their rooms are at home.
★ Teach the children the names of the colours of the rainbow by telling them the old saying, 'Richard Of York Gave Battle In Vain' – the initial letter of each word is the same as the initial letter of each colour of the rainbow.
★ Help the children to make their own colour book by writing a colour word on each page and drawing a variety of items that are associated with that colour. For example, on their 'green' page they could draw some grass, a plant leaf or the green light on a traffic-light.

Mathematical development
★ Cut out some card balloons and put a number on each one. Sit the children in a circle and give the balloons out randomly to them. Ask them to stand up in the right number order. Then invite the children to stand up if their number ends in a 2. Ask the child with the answer to 'add 1 and 2 together' to stand up.
★ In the rhyme, the mum is 'always painting things in the kitchen and the hall'. Encourage the children to make a pictogram that shows the colours of their kitchens. You may want to ask them to find out what colour their kitchen is the night before this activity.

Knowledge and understanding of the world
★ Talk to the children about different colours in their homes. Did they help to choose any of the paints used? Which is their favourite coloured room? Why?

Physical development
★ Provide the children with some paints and overalls and encourage them to paint an outside wall in your setting using big movements. You could even attempt to paint a design together such as a rainbow. If painting is not possible, try the same idea using buckets of water and practise making big arcs with the brushes.

Creative development
★ Help the children to make their very own rainbow painting. Provide them with a white sheet of paper, mixing palettes and a pot of water and invite them to experiment with mixing colours.

Early years wishing well: Me and my home

Rhymes

Who likes grapefruit?

Who likes grapefruit?
Who likes jam?
Who likes pizza?
Who likes ham?
Who likes apples?
Who likes cheese?
Who likes pancakes?
Who likes peas?
Who likes ice-cream
for their tea?
　Grandma,
　　Mum
　　　and
　　　　Dad
　　　　　and
　　　　　　me!

© Wes Magee

Rhymes

Who likes grapefruit?

Personal, social and emotional development

★ Create a pizza restaurant in your role-play area. Ask a local pizza takeaway to donate unused pizza boxes and serviettes. Make pizzas from cardboard circles and talk to the children about how half of a piece of pizza looks and how a quarter looks.

★ Ask the children to ask their friend what food they like and then report their answer back to the rest of the group.

Communication, language and literacy

★ Ask the children to draw each member of their family and to draw their favourite food next to them. Help the children to write the people's names next to the pictures.

★ Show the children how to write a shopping list using words or pictures.

★ Tell the children that 'Who likes jam?' is a question and that is why it has a question mark at the end.

★ Give each child a copy of the photocopiable sheet on page 81 and ask them to cut out the food words, match them to the correct pictures and then stick the words in place.

Mathematical development

★ Ask the children the same questions as in the rhyme, 'Who likes…?'. Count how many children like grapefruit and all the other foods mentioned such as apples.

Knowledge and understanding of the world

★ Invite the children to share their knowledge of where foods come from and where they are stored in a kitchen. If you can, show them visual examples of the food because some of the children may not know what a grapefruit, for example, looks like.

★ Ask the children to find out where either their grandma, their nearest or furthest relative lives.

Physical development

★ Ask if any of the children have tried grapefruit; did they like it? Talk about all types of fruit and how it is healthy for us to eat fruit and vegetables regularly. Are there any other fruits mentioned in the poem? Read it again and see if the children can recognize one (apples!).

Creative development

★ Show the children how food, such as potatoes, make great prints when dipped in paint. Use a square sponge and cut it into the shape of a house. The children could then print a repeating pattern, for example, house, potato, house.

★ Can the children clap the syllables in the food words? How many claps does the word grapefruit have?

★ Introduce percussion instruments and encourage the children to tap out or shake the rhythm of the word 'grapefruit'.

Early years wishing well: Me and my home

Stories

Tessa's new home

Tessa and her mum were moving to a new house today. They'd been packing all week and every room in the flat was full of boxes.

'Well, that's everything packed except the tea things,' said Mum. 'Now let's have a cup of tea before the removal men arrive.'

RIIING! RIIING! went the doorbell.

'Who's that?' asked Mum.

It was Mr Thomas from next door.

'I've come to wish you luck in your new home,' he said.

'Thank you,' said Mum. 'Would you like a cup of tea?'

'Yes, please,' said Mr Thomas.

Mum put the kettle on. 'It's a good job I haven't packed the tea-making things yet,' she said.

RIIING! RIIING! went the doorbell.

'Who's that?' asked Mum.

It was Susie and Aunt Mary from over the road.

'We've come to wish you luck in your new home,' they said.

'Thank you,' said Mum. 'Would you like a cup of tea?'

'Yes, please,' said Aunt Mary and Susie.

Mum got two more cups out and they all had a cup of tea.

RIIING! RIIING! went the doorbell.

'Who's that?' asked Mum.

It was the removal men.

'Are you all packed?' they asked.

'All except the tea things,' said Mum.

So Mr Thomas, Aunt Mary, Susie, Mum and Tessa all helped pack the furniture and boxes in the big van. Then the removal men got in the van and Mum and Tessa got in Mum's old car.

'Goodbye!' waved Mr Thomas, Aunt Mary and Susie. 'And good luck!'

'Goodbye!' waved Mum and Tessa.

Tessa felt really sad. She didn't want to leave her friends behind.

'I don't want to move to a new house with a garden,' she sniffed. 'I want to stay here with Mr Thomas, Aunt Mary and Susie.'

'I'll miss them, too,' said Mum. 'But they'll come and visit us, you'll see.'

Soon they were at the new house.

The removal men took all the furniture and boxes off the van and carried them into the house. Then they left.

Mum and Tessa were all alone.

Tessa felt sad.

'RIIING! RIIING!' went the bell.

'Who's that?' asked Mum.

It was Mr Thomas, Susie and Aunt Mary.

'We've come to help you unpack,' they all said.

'Thank you,' said Mum. 'Would you like a cup of tea?'

'Yes please,' they said.

Tessa smiled happily. 'Come and see our lovely new house,' she said. She wasn't sad now she knew that moving house didn't mean losing friends.

© Karen King

Early years wishing well: Me and my home

Stories

Tessa's new home

Personal, social and emotional development
★ Turn your role-play area into a house that needs packing up, just like Tessa's. Provide the children with lots of cardboard boxes and suitcases and invite them to re-enact the story. The area can become Tessa's new home once the removal men have arrived!
★ Encourage the children to discuss if their families have moved house. Ask them if they have any photographs of 'moving day'.

Communication, language and literacy
★ As you read the story to the children, ask them to think about how Tessa felt.
★ Tessa did not want to lose her friends in the story. Invite the children to make a special card for a friend that says 'Have a great day'.
★ Encourage the children to make a 'Good luck in your new home' card.
★ Ask the children to make a list of all their friends' names.

Mathematical development
★ Provide the children with a packed suitcase and ask them to find out how many T-shirts are inside.
★ Encourage the children to set a table, matching cups to saucers and a knife and a fork to each plate.
★ Invite the children to pair up. Ask the first child of each pair to throw a dice and to draw the corresponding number of houses on a wipeable board. Then ask the second child to count the number of houses to check that the correct amount was drawn. Finally, invite the pairs to wipe their board, swap their roles and start again.

Knowledge and understanding of the world
★ Challenge the children to find out which is the strongest material to carry ten books in. Provide them with paper, plastic, string, cotton and canvas bags to test.
★ Give the children a tray of soil and encourage them to make Tessa's new garden, using a variety of cuttings and little stones.

Physical development
★ Explain to the children that removal people have to be strong. Help them to exercise, showing them how to march on the spot, jog on the spot and do star jumps.
★ Ask the children to mime packing up boxes ready to move house, lifting heavy items and carefully placing lighter ones.

Creative development
★ Show the children how to hammer in wooden wheels to a block of balsa wood to create their own removal van. Invite them to find small objects to place on their van.
★ Invite the children to make their own house from a cereal box that has been turned inside out. Use a folded piece of card for the roof and cut out the windows and doors.

Early years wishing well: Me and my home

Stories

A new home for a mole?

A very small mole called Quentin Morrison Mole lived in a dark tunnel under the ground. Quentin's family had made tunnels in this part of the countryside for many years and they loved their home.

But Quentin wanted a change. He was tired of seeing the same dark holes all the time. He wanted to live outside, where there was a bright light called the sun and a great many colours. He knew about it all from his friend the glow-worm, who often shared their tunnel.

So one day, when the rest of the Morrison Moles were fast asleep, Quentin went in search of a new place to live.

It was a long way. But at last Quentin pushed and shoved the earth away and suddenly popped up from the middle of the little hill he had made. He blinked in the bright sunlight, and his nose could smell all kinds of wonderful things that were quite new to him. For Quentin had come up in the middle of a field of cows.

He scampered through the grass and fallen leaves. 'Brilliant!' he said. 'What a colourful home I could have here! No more dark tunnels for me!'

Suddenly, there was a swishing sound from above him and a dark shadow hid the sun. Quentin dived under a fallen log just as a large bird swooped over his head, and lay there trembling with fright.

Then Quentin felt the ground shake under him. Boom, boom, boom. Something huge was coming his way, with heavy, giant footsteps. It was a cow, looking for grass to eat, but Quentin didn't know that.

'Oh, no!' squeaked Quentin, and he ran back and dived into his hole in the ground. He kept running and running down one tunnel, then another, until he finally saw the light from his friend, glow-worm, and found his family still fast asleep.

Quentin snuggled up to his mother in their nest, his heart beating loudly from his fright. There were no giant birds or huge monsters down here, but only warm, safe darkness.

'This is the best home for moles,' thought Quentin, and he fell fast asleep.

© Ann Bryant

Stories

A new home for a mole?

Personal, social and emotional development
★ During circle time, encourage each child to say something that they like about their own home.
★ Ask the children to think about how they feel in the dark.

Communication, language and literacy
★ As you read the story to the children, ask them to think of some words that rhyme with 'day' such as 'way', 'hay', 'pay'.
★ Encourage the children to work as a group to make an animal alphabet book. Ask each child to do a page, choosing a letter, writing it and drawing a picture of an animal that begins with that letter.
★ Read the story through several times and encourage the children to clap their hands every time you reach a full stop.
★ Collect a variety of household objects such as a magazine, a mug, a plate, a spoon, and place them on a large tray. Ask the group to sit in a circle, and choose random children to select an object from the tray that begins with a particular sound, for example 'm'.

Mathematical development
★ Encourage the children to draw a picture of their house in the daytime showing the type of visitors and animals that they might see such as cats, dogs, postperson and milk deliverer. Next, they can do the same activity, this time showing their house at night-time with the animals that might be seen such as foxes and owls, and visitors such as a pizza delivery person.

Knowledge and understanding of the world
★ Ask the children to draw pictures of all the sources of light that they heard mentioned in the story, adding others that they know about from their own environment. These might include the sunlight that Quentin blinked in, traffic lights, torches and table lamps.
★ Make a table-top display of sources of light and invite the children to explore them.
★ Provide the children with a variety of tools to dig holes in your sand tray, just like Quentin Morrison Mole did!

Physical development
★ Create an obstacle course for the children in your outside area, with lots of tunnels for them to crawl through and objects for them to climb over.

Creative development
★ Let the children help you to create a collage display of animals that like to live underground, such as moles and badgers. Provide them with outlines of the animals and collage materials such as cotton wool, fur and sticky paper.
★ On rainy days, sing songs such as 'The Sun Has Got its Hat On'.

Leroy in a mood

Leroy's best friend, Jack, couldn't come round to play. Leroy felt fed up and cross and miserable all at the same time.

'What's the matter with Leroy?' his dad asked.

'He's in a mood,' said his mum. 'Leave him alone. He'll get over it.'

Leroy hadn't known he was in a mood – but being left alone sounded okay! His mum and dad were always on at him.

'Pick up your socks...', 'Don't tease the cat...', 'Have you brushed your teeth...?', 'Don't sniff...'.

Leroy had a bright idea. If being in a mood meant his mum and dad left him alone, perhaps he should try it.

'Leroy,' said his mum, 'help me carry the washing.'

'Shan't!' said Leroy. 'I'm in a mood.'

His mum game him a funny look but said nothing.

'Leroy, put these toys back in your box,' said his dad, 'before someone breaks their neck.'

'Shan't!' said Leroy. 'I'm in a mood.'

His dad opened his mouth wide – and then shut it.

'Come on,' said his mother at lunchtime, 'eat up your tomatoes. You know you like them.'

Leroy did, he loved them, but he was enjoying being in a mood more.

'Shan't!' he said. 'I'm in a mood.'

'Okay,' said his mum, and gave them to the cat.

Leroy scowled and stomped off to his room.

Later his mum called from the garden: 'It's lovely and sunny out here, Leroy. Bring your story-book down and I'll read it with you.'

'Shan't!' shouted Leroy. 'I'm in a mood.'

And to show he really meant it, he picked up the book and threw it out of the window! His mother glared up at him. Her face was bright red and her eyes were glinting. But she didn't come up after him ... weird!

Leroy was lying on his bed practising being in a mood when all at once the most beautiful smell drifted up from the patio. Smoky, sizzling beefburgers!

He raced downstairs.

'What are you doing?' he shouted to his mum and dad.

'We're having a barbecue tea,' said his dad. 'Grab a bun and come and get some.'

'Sha – ' he began to say. Then he licked his lips.

'Okay,' he said. 'I'm tired of being in a mood anyway. It's boring.'

And his mum and dad laughed.

© Patricia Leighton

Early years wishing well: Me and my home

Stories

Leroy in a mood

Personal, social and emotional development

★ Together with the children, practise making different faces to suit different moods. Start with a smile, then try an angry face, a sad face and a worried face. Develop this by asking the children to stand up and express their feelings using their whole bodies, for example hunching their shoulders to show that they are upset.

Communication, language and literacy

★ As you read the story to the children, encourage them to think about how Leroy felt in the story when he was in a mood. What feelings do they think his mum and dad were having?

★ Invite the children to help you write a list on your easel of all the feelings that we have, such as excitement, fear, worry, anger, sadness and stress.

Mathematical development

★ Do a survey among the children and find out how many like beefburgers. Make a simple bar chart to show the results.

★ Leroy had his barbecue on a patio. Give the children a template of a square and some brightly-coloured paper, and encourage them to cut out squares and stick them onto a piece of paper to create their own patio. Encourage the children to make sure that all the squares touch so that they tessellate together.

★ Read the story to the children again and this time ask them to count on their fingers how many times Leroy says 'I'm in a mood'.

Knowledge and understanding of the world

★ In the story, Leroy liked tomatoes. Grow your own in a growbag and encourage the children to help you water them regularly.

★ Invite the children to find out how food is cooked at home, for example, by gas, electrically in a microwave, or on a barbecue.

Physical development

★ Encourage the children to pretend to be the toys in Leroy's toy-box, for example, trains would make wheel movements with their hands and speed around, jack-in-the-boxes would jump up, once they are touched on their heads, and wave their hands from side to side (but they must be touched on their heads before they go back in their boxes) and teddies would move slowly taking giant steps.

Creative development

★ Encourage the children to look in a mirror and draw their face when they are smiling and when they are sad.

★ Copy the photocopiable sheet on page 82 onto card and cut out the cat shape. Give each child a copy of the cat and help them to attach a moveable tail to it with a paper fastener. Talk to the children about how cats show their feelings through using their tails.

Early years wishing well: Me and my home

Paul and the great big freezer

Paul's mum was a cook. She cooked at home for her job.

On Monday, Paul went into the kitchen to see what was for lunch.

'Steak and kidney puddings! Great!' said Paul.

'They're not for lunch, they're for the freezer,' said Paul's mum.

*And the great big freezer by the wall,
I kid you not, it winked at Paul.*

Paul scowled as he ate his beans on toast.

On Tuesday, Paul went into the kitchen to see what was for lunch.

'Chicken casseroles! Yum!' said Paul.

'They're for the freezer,' said Paul's mum.

*And the great big freezer by the wall
I kid you not, it winked at Paul.*

Paul scowled as he ate his fish fingers.

On Wednesday, Paul went into the kitchen to see what was for lunch.

'Tuna pastas! Brilliant!' said Paul.

'They're for the freezer!' said Paul's mum.

*And the great big freezer by the wall,
I kid you not, it winked at Paul.*

Paul scowled as he ate his tomato soup.

On Thursday, Paul went into the kitchen to see what was for lunch.

'Cheese and ham pies! Delicious!' said Paul.

'They're for the freezer,' said Paul's mum.

*And the great big freezer by the wall,
I kid you not, it winked at Paul.*

Paul scowled as he ate his spaghetti hoops.

On Friday, Paul helped his mum cooking. It was great fun until he began to feel hungry.

'What's for lunch, Mum? I'm starving,' said Paul.

'Just a sandwich, I'm afraid.'

Paul was furious.

'It's because that great big greedy freezer is going to have all the cooking, I suppose,' he snapped.

'No,' replied Paul's mum. 'Today, I'm going to take everything out of the freezer and deliver it to my customers.'

So Paul and his mum set to work.

When the freezer was completely empty, Paul heard a dripping noise. He looked at the freezer and saw little drips of ice tears spilling all down the front of it. Paul felt sorry for the freezer. So when his mum wasn't looking, he put a chicken casserole back into it.

*And the great big freezer by the wall,
I kid you not, it winked at Paul.*

And this time Paul winked back.

© Ann Bryant

Early years wishing well: Me and my home

Stories

Paul and the great big freezer

Personal, social and emotional development
★ During circle time, give the children the opportunity to say which is their favourite food. Talk about how people from different cultures like different foods and how some people can only eat certain foods.
★ Turn your role-play area into Paul's kitchen where the children can re-enact the story. Make a 'freezer' made from a large box painted white, with a face on the side.

Communication, language and literacy
★ While the children listen to the story, encourage them to think about which part keeps repeating itself. Write this phrase on a flip chart. Read the story again and encourage the children to join in at the repetitive bit.
★ Give each child a copy of the photocopiable sheet on page 83. Help them to cut out the freezer shape and then encourage them to use their memory to draw pictures of all the food that Paul's mum made during the week in the freezer. Fold down the flap to 'close' the freezer.

Mathematical development
★ Make a display of 'heavy foods' and 'light foods' and encourage the children to sort them into hoops by lifting them to decide if they are heavy or light.
★ Make a list of the days of the week and display it at the same height as the children. Using Blu-Tack, attach an arrow made out of card and invite a child to put the arrow on the correct day each morning.

Knowledge and understanding of the world
★ Put a balloon or some rubber gloves filled with water in a freezer. When solid, leave on a tray on the side and invite the children to watch them melt.
★ Help the children to make some sandwiches like Paul had to eat in the story. Make sure you use healthy fillings and remember to check on any special dietary requirements beforehand.

Physical development
★ Encourage the children to travel around the room in different ways such as crawling, jumping and skipping. Shout out the days of the week and tell the children they have to freeze when they hear Sunday. Change the pace of your voice when saying the words, sometimes going really fast and sometimes going really slowly.

Creative development
★ Make snow people by blowing up balloons and covering with papier mâché. Let them dry and then decorate with a smiley face. Cover a yoghurt pot with brown tape, add a cardboard disc to the bottom and paint it to create the snow person's hat. Tie a piece of crêpe paper around the neck to make a scarf.

Early years wishing well: Me and my home

Stories

Porridge and pictures

Mrs Atkins had told her class the story of 'Goldilocks and the Three Bears'. The children turned the home corner into the three bears' house. They filled three bowls with play dough.

'They are the three bowls of porridge,' said Hannah, who was Mother Bear.

They fetched three chairs.

'All the bears have chairs now,' said Jamie, who was Father Bear.

Finally, they put some cushions on the floor.

'Let's try the beds out,' said Kulvinder, who was Baby Bear. He jumped onto the cushions.

Then the bears went for their walk.

The children had fun taking it in turns to be Goldilocks finding the three bears' house and trying out the porridge, chairs and beds.

Then Mrs Atkins asked, 'What would Goldilocks see in *your* houses? Draw some pictures and show me.'

When they had finished, Mrs Atkins asked one or two children to hold up their pictures. Mark had drawn a lot of squares and rectangles with a ruler.

'What are all those shapes, Mark?' asked Mrs Atkins.

'That's the Play Station in my room,' said Mark, 'and these are my games. And that's my brother's computer and all his computer games.'

'That's a very neat picture,' said Mrs Atkins. 'I'm sure Goldilocks would like your house full of games.'

Gemma's picture was very bright – she had used a lot of colours, especially blue.

'What's all the blue, Gemma!' asked Mrs Atkins.

'It's the bluebells on the curtains in my mum's bedroom,' said Gemma. 'And the duvet cover that matches. And there are the stripy red blinds in my room.'

'It's a very bright picture,' said Mrs Atkins. 'I'm sure Goldilocks would like your house full of colour.'

Grace's picture was funny. There were two smiley faces and lots of red blobs and long squiggly bits.

'Tell us about your picture, Grace,' said Mrs Atkins.

'This is my little brother and me having tea in our kitchen,' said Grace. 'Mum has made some jam tarts.' She pointed to the red blobs.

'What are those long squiggly things?' asked Mrs Atkins.

'Worms,' said Grace. 'We like worms for tea!'

'Urgh!' cried the other children.

'Worms!' said Hannah, horrified.

'Goldilocks wouldn't like your house!' said Jamie.

'That's what my little brother calls spaghetti,' giggled Grace. 'It's our favourite.'

Everyone laughed. Then it was home time. They all tidied up the bears' house. While the children put on their coats, Mrs Atkins noticed that Kulvinder was still busy in the home corner.

'Time to go home, Kulvinder,' she reminded him.

'I'm just putting this out for Goldilocks, in case she visits the bears' house tonight,' he explained.

Mrs Atkins looked at the paper plate on the table, piled high with curly lengths of play dough.

'It's spaghetti,' said Kulvinder. 'In case she doesn't really like porridge.'

© Barbara Ball

Early years wishing well: Me and my home

Stories

Porridge and pictures

Personal, social and emotional development
★ Transform your home corner into the three bears' house. Make sure that the children help you to arrange all the props such as three bowls with play dough in for porridge, three chairs and so on. Encourage the children to take it in turns to be Goldilocks.

Communication, language and literacy
★ Read the story of 'Goldilocks and the Three Bears' (Traditional) to the children and ask them who their favourite character is.
★ Play the 'Word bingo game' using the photocopiable sheets on pages 84 and 85. Copy the 'Word bingo dice' (page 84) onto card, cut out the shape and fix it together. Make six copies of the 'Word bingo board' (page 85), laminate and place in plastic folders to provide a long-lasting resource. Put the cards face up on the table and give each child (six can play) a baseboard. Let the children throw the dice in turn, collect the appropriate card and match it to their board. Older children could spell out the words to the group. The winner is the one who collects all the words first and must shout 'House!'.

Mathematical development
★ Encourage the children to make a shape picture, like Mark did, using templates of two-dimensional shapes and sticky paper. Copy the photocopiable sheet on page 86 onto card and provide the children with shape templates and sticky coloured paper so that they can create their own shape pictures.
★ Ask the children to draw a picture of the bears in size order – shortest to tallest.

Knowledge and understanding of the world
★ Make porridge with small groups of children. Organize a tasting session and write down their responses such as 'delicious', 'yucky', 'yummy'.
★ Show the children some uncooked dried spaghetti, cook them away from the children and bring them back. Point out how they have changed into wriggly worms, as the children in the story call them!
★ Encourage the children to draw a map of the story of 'Goldilocks and the Three Bears' showing the cottage, the house where Goldilocks lived and the route that the bears took through the woods.

Physical development
★ Take a walk in your local environment, perhaps to the local park, just like the three bears, observing all the interesting features.

Creative development
★ Give each child a copy of the photocopiable sheet on page 87 and, using card and lolly sticks, ask them to make puppets of the characters. Invite them to re-enact the tale using their puppets.

Early years wishing well: Me and my home

That pup!

'Woof! Woof!' barked Benji, the new puppy, running off with Baby Jo's teddy bear. He took it to his basket and chewed its ear.

'Doggy!' laughed Baby Jo.

'Oh no!' groaned Harry.

'Oh no!' groaned Dad.

'Oh no!' groaned Mum. 'That pup will have to GO!'

'Woof!' barked Benji sadly.

Later, when they were all watching television, Benji suddenly grabbed Dad's tie.

'Grr! Grrr!' growled Benji, playfully, tugging at the tie.

'Stop it, Benji!' shouted Dad, trying to pull his tie away.

Dad pulled and Benji tugged. Then R..I..I..I..P! The tie ripped in half.

'Doggy!' laughed Baby Jo.

'Oh no!' groaned Harry.

'Oh no!' groaned Dad.

'Oh no!' groaned Mum. 'That pup will have to GO!'

'Woof!' barked Benji sadly.

The next day, Benji pulled the washing off the line. Socks, shirts and underpants were tossed all over the garden.

'Doggy!' laughed Baby Jo.

'Oh no!' groaned Harry.

'Oh no!' groaned Dad.

'Oh no!' groaned Mum. 'That pup's GOT to go!'

'Woof!' barked Benji sadly.

After lunch, Mum decided to go shopping. 'I'll take Harry and Baby Jo,' she said to Dad. 'We all need some fresh air.'

So Harry put his coat on while Mum put on Baby Jo's reins to stop her running away. Then off they went, out of the back door.

'Oh dear, I've forgotten my purse,' said Mum, turning back into the house. But just as Mum went in, Benji ran out.

'Woof! Woof!' barked Benji, running around and rolling in the mud.

'Doggy!' laughed Baby Jo.

'Oh no!' groaned Harry.

'Oh no!' groaned Dad.

'Oh no!' groaned Mum. 'That pup's got to go!'

Just then Harry saw that the garden gate was open, and Baby Jo was just about to walk out – right onto the main road.

'Oh no!' shouted Harry.

'Oh no!' shouted Dad.

'Oh no!' shouted Mum.

'Woof! Woof!' barked Benji, and he ran and grabbed Baby Jo's reins just as she was about to step into the road. 'Woof!' barked Benji, tugging at the reins to pull Baby Jo back into the garden.

'Doggy!' she laughed, and sat down PLONK on the grass.

'Well done, Benji!' smiled Harry.

'Well done, Benji!' smiled Dad.

'Well done, Benji!' smiled Mum. 'I think this pup can stay.'

'Woof!' barked Benji, happily.

© Karen King

Early years wishing well: Me and my home

Stories

That pup!

Personal, social and emotional development

★ Ask the children to bring in a photograph of their pet (if they have one) and describe it to the rest of the children. Make a display of the photographs.

★ In your home corner, set up an animal hospital with soft toys as patients and provide bandages and other equipment. Encourage the children to take it in turns to be the vet or the animals' owners.

★ In the story, Benji pulled the washing line down. Encourage the children to help you do some washing in your setting such as washing the dolls' clothes.

Communication, language and literacy

★ As you read the story to the children, encourage them to join in the repetitive part of the text. Make sure that they use expression in their voices.

★ Encourage the children to think of phrases that they could say to the dog to praise him, rather than saying 'Oh no!' every time. Write the children's responses on a flip chart, for example, 'good dog' or 'what a clever dog'.

Mathematical development

★ Benji ripped the dad's tie in half. Show the children how to fold a piece of paper in half, and on the fold draw half of a heart. Keeping the paper folded, ask them to cut out their shape and then fold it out into a whole heart.

★ Give the children some Plasticine and invite them to make a cake. Then encourage them to give half to their friend.

★ Give each child a copy of the photocopiable sheet on page 88 and ask them to choose two colours to create a repeating pattern, such as stripes.

Knowledge and understanding of the world

★ Show the children pictures of animals and encourage them to imitate the sound that each animal makes.

Physical development

★ Encourage the children to travel on all fours, just like Benji does in the story. Can they move fast and slowly? Can they think of any other ways that animals travel, such as snakes slithering on their bellies?

Creative development

★ Using rolled-up newspaper and brown tape, help the children to make their own puppy. When it is finished, glue on brown tissue paper and black sticky paper to represent the face.

Early years wishing well: Me and my home

Information text

A favourite place

I love my bedroom. It's the place I like best in the whole of our flat. This is where I play my favourite games, do jigsaws, put out my train set and read my books. It's extra special because *I* chose all the colours and everything, right down to the quilt on my bed!

When I was a tiny baby, Mum and Dad decorated my room with pink wallpaper with blue teddy bears all over it. But later, when I was bigger, I said that I'd like my room to be like a spaceship, travelling through space.

I helped Mum take off all the old wallpaper (that was hard work!) and paint the walls dark blue. We bought a new, grey carpet. Then we stuck stars on the ceiling that shone in the dark, and I made a paper moon to hang over the light.

My bed has a duvet with rockets and spaceships all over it, and it matches the curtains at the window.

When I lie in bed, I think I am a starship captain, and my teddy bear and other toys are my crew.

Every night, when the light goes out, I look up at the stars and think about where we might travel tonight. 'Start the engines,' I whisper, 'and head for that star on the right...'.

© Stevie Ann Wilde

Early years wishing well: Me and my home

Information text

A favourite place

Personal, social and emotional development
★ Encourage the children to talk about their own bedrooms, telling the others why they like it and how it is decorated.
★ In pairs, let the children tell a partner about some of the dreams that they have had.

Communication, language and literacy
★ Encourage the children to listen carefully to every detail of the text, then to draw a picture of the bedroom described, labelling it with sounds such as 's' for stars. Now ask them to draw a picture of their own bedrooms and then label them in the same way.
★ Encourage the children to make a list of some of the items they have in their room.

Mathematical development
★ Encourage the children to count from zero to ten and from ten to zero, to practise the launch of their rockets.
★ In turn, ask the children to show you ten fingers and count each one.
★ Count in ones with the children, but this time they have to alternate with you, for example, you say one, and the children say two and so on.
★ Give each child a copy of the photocopiable sheet on page 89 and ask them to trace the numbers and draw the correct number of circles in each section of the rocket.

Knowledge and understanding of the world
★ Encourage the children to look up at the stars and moon at night, over a period of a month. Ask them to recognize and talk to their parents about how the moon changes during the month.
★ Create a 'bedroom materials table' with different samples of carpet for the children to feel, and different textures of wallpaper.

Physical development
★ Put on some twinkling music such as 'Merry Christmas, Mr Lawrence' by Ryuichi Sakamoto (EMI Virgin Music Ltd, 1993, Milan Records) and encourage the children to twinkle and turn, making star shapes on their own and with a partner.

Creative development
★ Encourage the children to each make a rocket using newspaper and wallpaper paste. Cover a washing-up bottle with papier mâché and cut off the bottom of the bottle. When the papier mâché is hard, let the children paint the rocket and stick orange and yellow tissue paper at the bottom edge so it looks as if it is taking off.
★ Make shoebox models of the children's bedrooms, using smaller boxes for wardrobes and beds. Provide the children with catalogues and invite them to cut out some of the items that they have in their bedroom and stick them inside their model.

Early years wishing well: Me and my home

Information text

New shoes

My old shoes were horrid! They didn't look very nice any more, and they pinched my toes.

Mum said it was time I had some new ones. We went to a shoe shop in town to buy them. The lady put my feet on a kind of ruler to see how long my feet were. Then she measured round them with a tape to see how wide they were. She asked what kind of shoes I wanted.

'I need some shoes to go to nursery school,' I said.

First, I tried on some red sandals. I didn't like the colour.

Next, I tried on some trainers, but I couldn't tie up the long laces.

Then, I tried some shoes that had thick rubber soles covered with animal footprints. But they were too heavy.

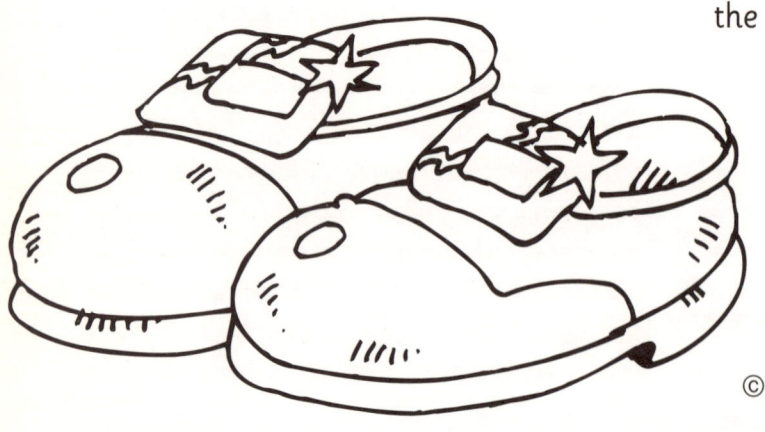

Then, I put on some blue shoes with shiny buckles. I liked the colour. I walked up and down the carpet in them and looked in the funny mirror that only showed my feet. The shoes were very comfy. 'These are just right,' I said. The shop lady said how nice they looked. Mum said she liked them, too. So we bought them.

'Shall I put them in the box for you?' asked the lady.

I looked at my old shoes. They looked so scruffy I really didn't want to put them on again. I thought of the shiny blue new pair.

'Would you like to wear the new ones instead?' asked Mum.

I nodded. 'Yes, please.'

Mum put my old shoes in the box instead and we went home. And all the way, I couldn't help looking down at my feet, at my new blue shoes with silvery buckles. Right, left, right, left. In, out, up and down. Point, skip, point, skip. 'JUST LOOK AT MY NEW SHOES, EVERYBODY!'

© Stevie Ann Wilde

Information text

New shoes

Personal, social and emotional development

★ Set up a shoe shop in your role-play area. Supply plenty of pairs of shoes for the children to try on, boxes to pack the shoes in, and paper and pencils for the children to draw around people's feet. If you can, provide real money for the children to use in the shoe shop.

★ Encourage the children to talk about the last time that they had a new pair of shoes bought for them. Ask them if they know how the shop assistant found out their shoe size.

Communication, language and literacy

★ Using the text, encourage the children to tell you the words that were used to describe the old shoes and the new shoes.

★ Help the children to make their own information book about shoes. Provide the vocabulary for different types of shoes such as 'trainers', 'boots' and 'sandals'. Show them how to write the name of a shoe type on each page and then cut pictures from magazines and catalogues that they can stick on their headed pages.

Mathematical development

★ Let the children use their feet as a form of measurement. Show them how to measure the room carefully going from heel to toe and so on.

★ Encourage the children to measure tables using their hand span.

★ Using two large hoops, ask the children to sort a selection of shoes using the criteria that you set them, such as red shoes in one hoop, not red shoes in the other.

Knowledge and understanding of the world

★ Gather the children into a circle and place a variety of shoes in the middle. Encourage the children to think about why we wear certain footwear in certain types of weather and invite them to comment on when each type of shoes are worn. For example, we wear wellington boots when it is raining so that we keep our feet dry.

★ Encourage the children to look at all the different types of shoes that they have in their home, such as boots and trainers.

Physical development

★ Encourage the children to pretend to put on a certain type of footwear and then move appropriately. They may start jumping in puddles if they have on pretend wellington boots or jogging around the room if they have on pretend trainers.

Creative development

★ Give the children some card, yoghurt pots and fabric to make their own pairs of shoes. Show them how to draw around their own feet on the card, how to stick the yoghurt pots to make heels, and how to arrange the fabric to make straps.

Early years wishing well: Me and my home

Information text

My rabbit

I have a pet rabbit called Biscuit. I called her that because she is a light brown colour. She has thick, soft fur, long ears that stand up straight, and a brown nose that twitches all the time. I try to twitch my nose, too, but I can't do it as well as Biscuit!

When we got Biscuit at the pet shop she was very small, but we bought her a large hutch, to give her lots of room for when she grew bigger, and my dad made a special run for her so she can play on the lawn and nibble the grass when the weather is nice.

Biscuit spends most of her time nibbling. I give her fruit, vegetables and special bunny food. And she always has clean water.

Every day, I help to clean her hutch. We take out all the dirty straw and any food she hasn't eaten, and put in clean straw and curly wood shavings.

Biscuit comes into the house as well. I play a game of hiding some of her bunny nibbles under the sofa cushions or in a cardboard box, and she hops round trying to find them all. She likes me to brush her coat with a soft brush, but best of all she loves to be cuddled.

My little brother will soon be old enough to have a pet too, so we will be able to get Biscuit a friend to be with. I hope he'll choose another rabbit, but he says he wants a guinea-pig. Biscuit won't mind, because we will still be best friends.

© Jackie Andrews

Early years wishing well: Me and my home

Information text

My rabbit

Personal, social and emotional development
★ Invite a real-life fluffy rabbit to your setting! Ask its owner to show the children how it moves. Ensure that it is not too timid and does not mind being stroked. Ask the children to observe the rabbit and watch what it does.
★ Encourage the children to think about how their home is different from the one that an animal lives in. Do they have straw on their mattress? Do animals have a bedroom, a bathroom and a kitchen?

Communication, language and literacy
★ As you read the text to the children, encourage them to listen to every detail. At the end, allow them to share their own experiences of rabbits.
★ Help the children to make their own information book about rabbits. Provide them with paper cut in the shape of a rabbit. On the first page, encourage them to draw and write about what rabbits look like, then on the other page, to draw and write about where rabbits live, what they eat, what people must do to look after them and what they like to do. Place the finished books in your book corner so that the children can share them.
★ Ensure that you have a good variety of information books about animal habitats in your book corner.

Mathematical development
★ Encourage the children to measure the circumference of their own head and to make a headband out of card, attaching cardboard rabbit ears to it.
★ Make a pictogram of all the pets that the children have. Encourage them to each draw a picture of their own pet and then stick it in the appropriate column.

Knowledge and understanding of the world
★ Encourage the children to think about the different ways that we care for animals. Provide them with props such as food bowls, leads and cushions to stimulate their thinking. Let them choose an animal, draw it and then draw all the things that it needs around it.
★ Ask the children to think about which animal they would like to have living in their home. Would they like a cat or a snake?

Physical development
★ Encourage the children to do bunny hops along the floor and then along different pieces of equipment, such as benches.

Creative development
★ Provide the children with a large box and encourage them to make their own hutch for a rabbit. Provide them with real straw to put inside and cut out holes for the pets to see through. They could make their own rabbit, using rolled-up newspaper and brown tape.

Early years wishing well: Me and my home

Information text

Delivering the food

My dad drives a big lorry and delivers food to lots of supermarkets. He delivers the food at night so that the supermarket workers can fill the shelves ready for people to do their shopping in the morning. So Dad goes out to work when I go to bed. Mum makes him a flask of tea and some sandwiches and Dad sets off for the night.

'Where are you going tonight, Dad?' I ask. Sometimes he says Scotland or London or Wales. Sometimes he says places that I've never heard of. As I lie in bed, I think of my dad driving his big lorry. This is what my dad told me he does at work.

First, Dad has to put all the boxes of food in the back of the lorry. He uses a big trolley thing on wheels to do this. When the lorry is full, Dad sets off. He drives through the night, along the motorway. When he reaches the supermarket, Dad drives around to the back where everything is kept before it's put on the shelves. He takes all the boxes for that supermarket off the lorry and someone takes them into the big stockroom. They check that Dad has brought everything they ordered. Dad drives off again to another supermarket. After a few hours, Dad stops for something to eat and a rest before he drives to the next supermarket. When all the food has been delivered, Dad drives the lorry back, ready for another driver to use. Then he gets in his car and comes home. Dad gets home just as I get up. He looks very tired but he smiles and says good morning to me. He has a cup of tea and goes to bed. And that's how my Dad delivers the food to the supermarkets.

© Karen King

photocopiable

Early years wishing well: Me and my home

Information text

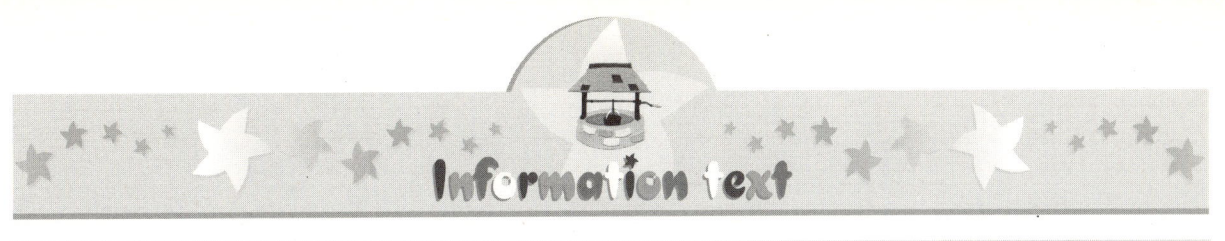

Delivering the food

Personal, social and emotional development

★ Encourage the children to talk about what their parents do for a job. Ask them to give as many details as possible, for example, what tasks they have to do, what time they come back home, and so on. Remain sensitive to individual circumstances.

★ Some parents may be prepared to come in and talk to the children about what they do each day, and what they have to wear for their job. There may be a parent who works at the local supermarket who could talk to the children, for example.

Communication, language and literacy

★ After you have read the text to the children, use a large children's atlas to find the places mentioned such as Scotland or London.

★ Encourage the children to share any information that they have about supermarkets. Did they know that somebody has to deliver the food to the supermarket and that sometimes it comes a long distance? Have they seen people working at the supermarket stacking the shelves and working on the tills?

Mathematical development

★ Set up a supermarket in your home corner and allow the children to use real money. Interact with them, using correct vocabulary such as 'How much is this, please?'.

★ Reinforce daytime and night-time by asking the children if any of their parents have to work during the night.

Knowledge and understanding of the world

★ Arrange for the children to visit the local supermarket and find out how it is run. They may even be allowed to see the stockroom. Look at the shops that you pass on the way and notice if anyone lives above them. Encourage the children to think about why people live above shops. How do they get into their homes?

★ Ask the children to find out where food is stored in their own home. Do they have a food cupboard, fridge, freezer? How often do their parents go to the supermarket?

Physical development

★ Play the 'bean game' with the children responding with actions to the type of bean that you call out. For example, when you say 'runner bean', the children run on the spot, when you say 'baked bean', they lie down and sunbathe, when you say 'chilli bean', they stand on the spot and shiver, and when you say 'French bean', they do the cancan.

Creative development

★ Recreate your own local street using cereal boxes and shoe boxes. Help the children to paint on the shop signs and windows of the flat above, if there is one.

Early years wishing well: Me and my home

Information text

Going shopping by the sea

We live in a house by the seaside. Today, we are going shopping for something for tea. Mum puts baby Amy in the pushchair, gets her purse and shopping bag and we set off. I hold on to the pushchair too, because our street is very steep and made of cobblestones. Amy loves it when her pushchair bumps over them.

Because it is summertime, there are lots of people about. They are eating ice-creams, fish and chips, and stopping to take photos. Mum says they are on holiday. I can't understand what some of them say, and Mum says they're from another country. I feel very pleased that people want to come here for their holidays, but I wish they wouldn't all come at once. It takes ages to get to the shops. (In winter, it's different. Not many people come because it's cold and windy here, and the sea is too rough for people to swim in it.)

Our first stop is at the harbour to buy some fresh fish. I like it at the harbour. It's full of lovely sounds and smells. I like to look at the boats and to watch the seagulls.

Two people are sitting on a bench eating fish and chips. A cheeky seagull flies down, grabs a chunk of fish in its beak, and flies off with it. I laugh. I like seagulls. They are funny.

At the other end of the harbour is the fish shop. There are lots of different sorts of fish. I like the tubs of mussels, prawns and crab sticks best. Mum buys some fish and a crab stick for Amy and me. Then we go up the hill to the supermarket. It's a very steep hill so I help Mum push Amy's pushchair. At the supermarket, Mum buys some bread, potatoes and carrots.

On the way home, we see a lady pretending to be a statue outside the tea-shop. She is painted in gold and wears gold clothes. She stands very still. Lots of people are watching her and throw some money into a hat that she has put on the floor. When I first saw the lady I thought she *was* a statue, until she moved just a little bit.

We see a man selling jewellery and a lady plaiting someone's hair with different coloured wool.

Then we see our house. Our shopping trip is over.

© Karen King

photocopiable

Early years wishing well: Me and my home

Information text

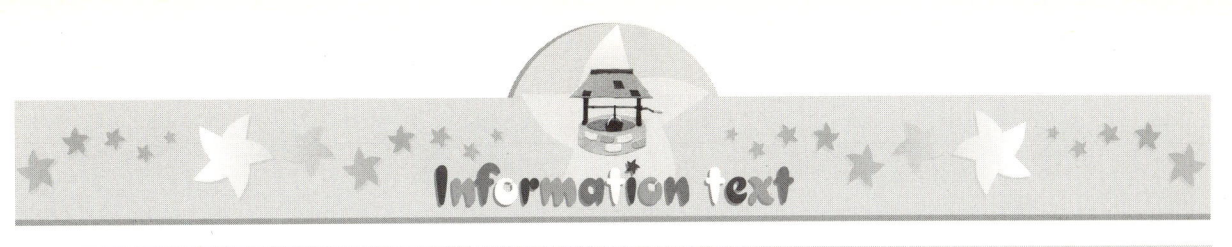

Going shopping by the sea

Personal, social and emotional development
★ Ask the children to pair up and invite each child to tell their partner about their last shopping trip.
★ Have a holiday circle time: encourage each child to tell the others about the 'home' that they stayed in when they were last on holiday. Invite them to help you make a list of the different types of homes, such as caravan, tent, cottage, house, flat.

Communication, language and literacy
★ Encourage the children to listen carefully to the text and think about what is near to their house. It may be a park or busy street or perhaps the seaside.
★ Ask the children why they think there is a fish shop at the end of the harbour. What did the little girl most like to eat? Do they like eating fish?
★ Help the children to create a postcard. Encourage them to imagine that they are on holiday, like the people in the story in the girl's home town. They could draw the naughty seagull on the front of the card, and a short message, or just their name, on the other side.

Mathematical development
★ Show the children how to make a season wheel. Take a disc of card and divide it into four segments. Draw a picture for each season in each quarter. Fix a cardboard arrow to the centre and encourage the children to make it point to the appropriate season. Explain to the children that the seasons are a cycle and are continuous.

Knowledge and understanding of the world
★ Think about the area in which you live. Ask the children to consider why they like the area and why they don't. Ask them, 'If you had one wish to live anywhere in the world, where would it be?'.
★ Invite the children to draw a map to show their house and the route that they take when they go shopping.

Physical development
★ Play statues with the children. Encourage them to pretend that they are doing something at home or that they are walking in the local area. Tell them that when you shout 'freeze', they should stand very still and not move.
★ When playing games with the children, always encourage them to use every bit of space in the room but also to be aware of everybody else around them.

Creative development
★ Encourage the children to colour dried pasta with felt-tipped pens or paints and then thread them onto wool to create necklaces and bracelets.

Early years wishing well: Me and my home

My house

My house, my house, my house is a spe-cial house.

My house, my house, my house is where I live.

1. Well it may be a big house, it may be small, It may be a bun-ga-low with just one floor. It may be a car-a-van, it may be a flat But my house is where I live.

2. Well it may be an old house, it may be new. It may have a lot of rooms or on-ly two. It may be a yel-low house, it may be blue But my house is where I live.

© Clive Barnwell

58
photocopiable

Early years wishing well: Me and my home

Songs

My house

Personal, social and emotional development

★ Give each child a special day. Encourage them to bring in three special objects from home and place them on a designated special table. Let them wear a badge that says, 'I'm special', and give them special responsibilities in your setting that day. Do not forget to give yourself a special day as well – the children will love to see your objects.

★ Copy the photocopiable sheet on page 90 for each child and keep it in a safe place. Fill out a copy of the special letter for each child as required.

Communication, language and literacy

★ Invite the children to help you write a list of all the types of homes that are mentioned in the song, such as house, bungalow and caravan. Encourage them to think about any other lists that you could write, such as the colours that their houses are painted.

★ Create a writing table in your setting and leave on it a variety of writing materials and paper that is cut in the shape of a house to stimulate the children to write.

Mathematical development

★ Ask the children to count the number of floors, of rooms, of beds and of chairs that they have in their house. Does the number of beds match the amount of people who live in their house?

Knowledge and understanding of the world

★ Make a table-top display of old and new household objects. Encourage the children to observe the differences, such as the materials used. Ask them to think about how we should treat old objects and what it feels like when they have new things.

★ Encourage the children to find out if they have ever been on holiday in a caravan. Where did they go? Did they enjoy living in a caravan? What are the differences between a house and a caravan? Would they like to live in a caravan permanently?

★ Using a paint program on your computer, encourage the children to draw a picture of their house using the mouse. Show them how to print out their picture and display all the drawings in your computer corner.

Physical development

★ Encourage the children to make big and small movements on the climbing equipment.

Creative development

★ Sing the song to the children first so that they can listen to it and get the idea of the tune. Then sing a line at a time to them, with them repeating it back so that you begin to develop their memory of it.

★ Encourage the children to think of actions that they can do while they sing the song, such as draw a picture of a house in the air when they sing 'my house'.

Early years wishing well: Me and my home

Songs

That's my chair!

(Tune: 'Three Blind Mice')

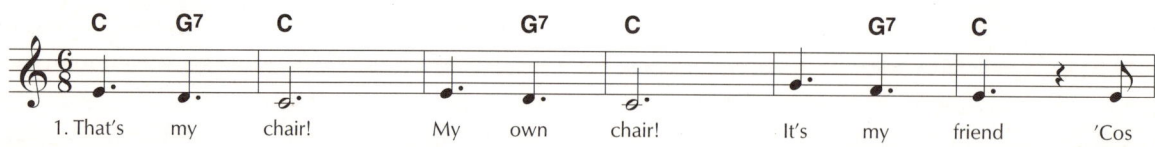

1. That's my chair! My own chair! It's my friend 'Cos I can pretend, I'm driving fast in a racing car,* Or zooming through space to a far-off star,* And sometimes I sit and just laugh, "ha, ha, ha,"* In my own chair.

2. That's my bed!
My own bed!
It's my friend
'Cos I can pretend,
I'm in a cave watching dinosaurs,
Or shadows that creep up the walls and doors,
And lying so still when the wind howls and roars*
In my own bed.

3. That's my box!
My own box!
It's my friend
'Cos I can pretend,
It's full of treasure from pirate ships,
And creatures so strange they have zips for lips,
And all of my most precious things I keep
In my own box.

© Peter Morrell

*Appropriate actions/sound effects can be added!

Early years wishing well: Me and my home

Songs

That's my chair!

Personal, social and emotional development
★ Create a cave in your home corner and invite the children inside to sit on comfortable cushions and read stories. Provide soft dinosaurs and a box of treasures to stimulate their imagination.
★ Encourage the children to talk about where they like to sit and think. You may even like to designate a chair in your room that children can go to when they just want to think.

Communication, language and literacy
★ Present a tray of treasures to the children and let them study them carefully. Take the tray away and remove one object. Bring the tray back and ask the children to try and recall which object is missing.

Mathematical development
★ Provide the children with outlines of two-dimensional shapes that they can draw around to create a shape picture. For example, they may want to draw a picture of themselves in a racing car zooming through space to a far-off star.
★ As the children draw around the shapes, encourage them to count the edges.

Knowledge and understanding of the world
★ Arrange to borrow an overhead projector from your local primary or secondary school. Set it up with white paper on a wall and ask the children to sit profile on in front of the projector with the paper behind them. Draw around the children's outlines, which are cast onto the white paper, with a black marker pen. You could then transfer the outline onto a black piece of paper so that the children have their very own silhouette.
★ Ask the children to go home and research which chair they find to be the most comfortable. They can do this by performing a comfort test in as many chairs as possible around their house. Back in your setting, encourage the children to discuss the differences and similarities they found between chairs.

Physical development
★ If you are able to, invest in large bikes and cars on which the children can develop their large motor skills.

Creative development
★ Teach the children the words of the song 'That's my chair'. Encourage them to think of their own sound effects that they can add when performing the song.
★ Help the children to make a chair for their favourite teddy bear or doll. Collect two boxes and turn them inside out, resealing them with brown tape. Collect four tubes and attach them to the bottom of one of the boxes. Attach the other box so that it is the backrest for the chair.

Early years wishing well: Me and my home

My jobs

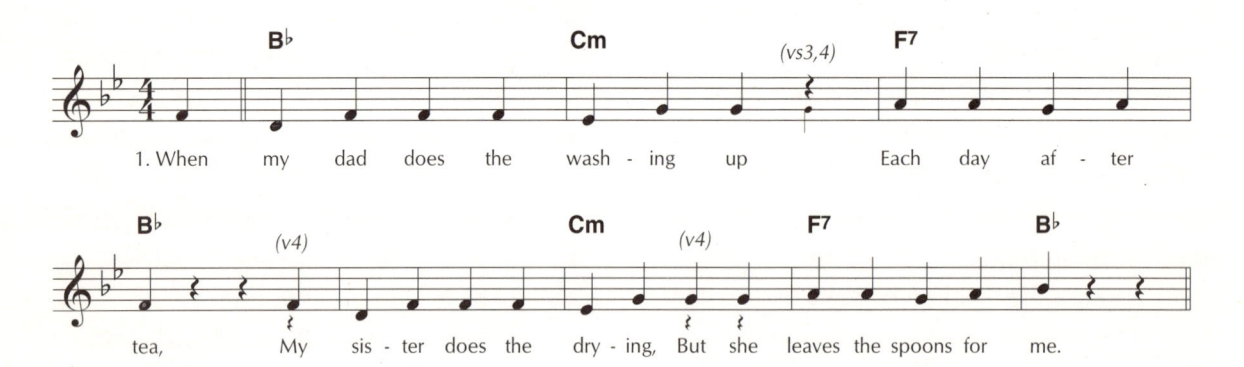

1. When my dad does the washing up
Each day after tea,
My sister does the drying,
But she leaves the spoons for me.

2. When Mummy puts the washing out
On the washing line,
I hand her all the plastic pegs
Because that job is mine.

3. When Grandad goes to wash the car,
To make it gleam and shine,
He never, never cleans the wheels,
Because that job is mine.

4. When Gran has lost her glasses,
That she wears to help her see,
Who's the one who finds them?
Yes, you've guessed. It's ME!

© Susan Eames

Follow-up activities:
Talk about any jobs that the children do at home.
Mime the jobs mentioned in the song.
One child mimes an activity in the song, and the others try to guess it.

Early years wishing well: Me and my home

Songs

My jobs

Personal, social and emotional development
★ Turn your role-play area into a variety of work situations such as a hairdresser's (without scissors); a launderette, with cardboard boxes acting as washing machines and dryers, and suitcases for sorting clothes and packing them back into; a car park, where the children can park toy cars and make garages out of Lego to carry out general maintenance.
★ Make a list of jobs that need doing at your setting and encourage the children to take responsibility for some of them.
★ Invite the children to talk about the jobs that they do at home and why it is important to be helpful.

Communication, language and literacy
★ Write the words of the song onto a flip chart and ask the children to read it with you and identify the words that rhyme together.
★ Invite the children to help you to write a list of words that rhyme with 'dad'.

Mathematical development
★ Ask the children to sort cars by colour and put them into sets by counting them.
★ Ask them how many jobs 'me' in the song does and how many people are mentioned.
★ Encourage the children to count how many people are in their families and to draw them inside a house outline in height order.
★ Show the children a number card. Ask them to give you the card with the number just below or the one with the number just above it.
★ Give the children the number cards (0-10) in a pile and ask them to place them in order on the floor, starting with either 0 or 10.

Knowledge and understanding of the world
★ Encourage the children to think about what job they would like to do when they grow up and why.
★ Ask parents or members of the local community if they would like to come in and talk to the children about their job and any special clothes they have to wear when they are working.

Physical development
★ Encourage the children to think of some jobs and then act them out. Clap your hands and ask the children to freeze, then walk around and guess what job they are doing.

Creative development
★ Copy the photocopiable sheet on page 91 onto card and make a pair of cardboard glasses for each child to wear as they sing the verse about Grandma.
★ Make a washing line out of two carboard tubes and a piece of string between them. Allow the children to peg different squares of materials on their washing line.

Early years wishing well: Me and my home

Out in my back garden

(Tune: 'The Big Ship Sails')

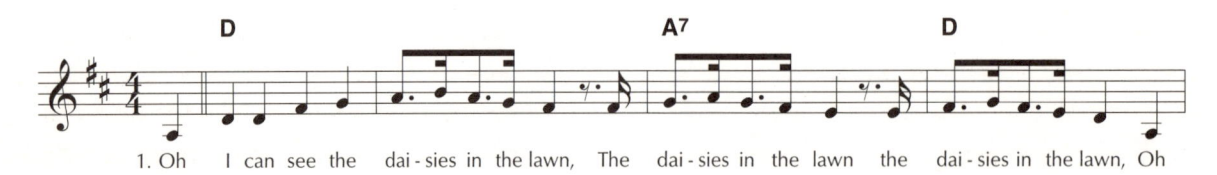

1. Oh I can see the daisies in the lawn, The daisies in the lawn the daisies in the lawn, Oh I can see the daisies in the lawn When I'm out in my back garden.

2. Oh I can help my mum to pull up weeds,
My mum to pull up weeds, my mum to pull up weeds,
Oh I can help my mum to pull up weeds
When I'm out in my back garden.

3. Oh I can see the pansies in the pots…

4. Oh I can help my dad to rake the soil…

5. Oh I can see the weeping willow tree…

Add other verses of your own.

© Ann Bryant

Songs

Out in my back garden

Personal, social and emotional development
★ Create your own garden centre in the home corner. It could sell artificial flowers, plant pots and small gardening tools, and even have an area where people can have a drink and cake. As an alternative to a sand tray, provide a tray of peat for the children to explore and dig in.

Communication, language and literacy
★ Copy the photocopiable sheet on page 91 onto card and give each child a daisy and a strip of card. Ask the children to draw around the daisy on white paper and cut it out. Let the children practise how to form the letter 'd' in the middle of each daisy and then stick them onto their strip of card. Help younger children by writing the letter 'd' in yellow felt-tipped pen so that they can trace over it. When they have lots of daisies on their card, staple the ends so that it becomes their own crown of daisies.
★ Let the children make a flower card for someone of their own choice. Help them to write a message or their name in it.

Mathematical development
★ Provide the children with a variety of plant pots and encourage them to put them in size order from the smallest to the biggest.
★ Copy the photocopiable sheet on page 92 onto card. Cut up the cards as shown and give one to each child. Ask them to count how many flowers they can see on the cards and then how many petals.

Knowledge and understanding of the world
★ Show the children a vase of flowers and encourage them to observe them growing in your immediate environment. Talk to the children about when you are allowed to cut flowers and when you are not, such as when you are walking in the countryside.

Physical development
★ In a large open space, ask the children to pretend that they are seeds floating in the air. Once they have taken root, go around pretending to water each of them. Talk to the children as they act out growing like a flower and then waving in the breeze.

Creative development
★ Put a large vase of flowers on your art table and ask the children to paint what they see. Invite them to pay particular attention to the colours.
★ Create a changing tree in your setting by changing its branches according to the passing seasons, using collage materials. For example, in the spring, add buds made out of small balls of tissue paper. In the summer, turn these into flowers. In the autumn, have only a few branches with yellow and orange leaves, and in the winter, have bare branches.

Growing

2. If I eat my lunch
I will grow up big and strong,
So I'll eat up all my sandwiches
And sing this song.

3. If I eat my tea
I will grow up big and strong,
So I'll eat up all my fish and chips
And sing this song.

4. If I eat my greens
I will grow up big and strong,
So I'll eat up all my broccoli
And sing this song.

5. If I eat my fruit
I will grow up big and strong,
So I'll eat up all my pear and grapes
And sing this song.

6. If I drink my milk
I will grow up big and strong,
So I'll drink up all my milk today
And sing this song.

*Stretch up tall on 'big and strong'.

© Johanne Levy

Songs

Growing

Personal, social and emotional development

★ Organize a fruit time each day, with the children selecting fruit from a plate that is passed around.

★ Create a fish and chip shop in your home corner. Encourage the children to paint fish onto card and cut chips out of yellow card to serve in the shop. Provide newspaper for the children to roll up into cones and to serve the fish and chips in.

Communication, language and literacy

★ Encourage the children to help you write a menu that can be displayed in the fish and chip shop. You could also write prices for each item on the menu.

★ Play 'I like to eat something beginning with "p"' with the children, encouraging them to predict all the food that they know that begins with 'p' such as pizza, peas, pears and plums. Try the game again, using other letters of the alphabet.

Mathematical development

★ Display a huge outline of a growing tree and mark the children's height on it on a regular basis, making a small line and the name for each child.

★ Create a sorting table with two large hoops, a variety of objects and two signs saying, 'big' and 'small'. Ask the children to sort different objects into the correct hoops.

Knowledge and understanding of the world

★ Help the children to make a fruit salad. Tell them that it will help them to grow and be healthy. Provide them with a variety of soft fruit and some blunt knives to chop the fruit. Add orange juice to the fruit salad and serve into bowls. Alternatively, make fruit kebabs. Enjoy together at snack time.

★ Sit the children in a circle and pass a variety of fruit around. Encourage them to smell and touch the fruit. Introduce some unusual fruit which the children have not seen before.

Physical development

★ Sit the children in a circle and play a fun healthy food game. Name three children 'milk', 'pear' and 'apple' then repeat around the circle, until all of the children have a name. Then say, 'All the children who are called milk, can you crawl across the circle to someone else's space'. 'If you are an apple can you jump across the circle and sit down in someone else's place'.

Creative development

★ Give the children a paper plate and some collage materials. Encourage them to use these to make their favourite healthy meal such as chicken, peas and potatoes.

★ Cut some fruit in half and invite the children to make accurate drawings of what they can see inside. Let them use coloured pencils to carefully shade in the drawings.

Early years wishing well: Me and my home

Looking after ourselves

(Tune: 'Row, Row, Row your Boat')

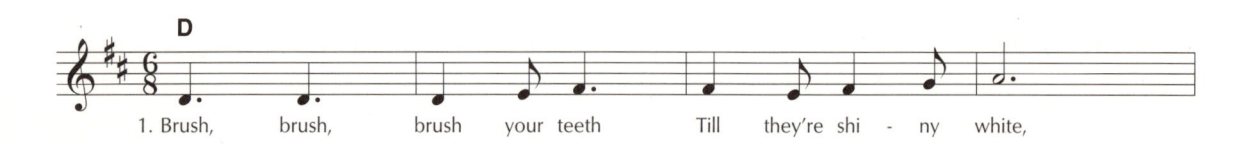

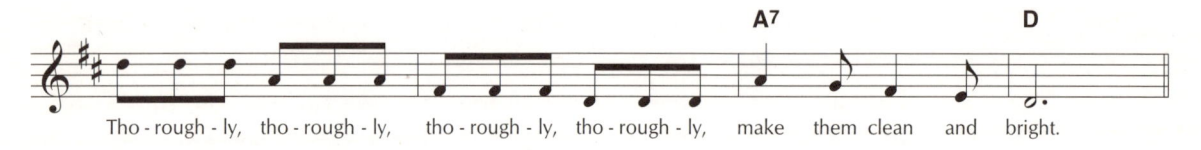

1. Brush, brush, brush your teeth
Till they're shiny white,
Thoroughly, thoroughly, thoroughly, thoroughly,
Make them clean and bright.

(Action: Children move hand up and down, pretending to brush teeth)

2. Comb, Comb, Comb your hair
Till it's tangle free,
Tidily, Tidily, Tidily, Tidily,
Now do you see?

(Action: Children pretend to comb hair)

3. Wash, Wash, Wash your face
Wash away the dirt,
Carefully, Carefully, Carefully, Carefully,
Now the germs won't hurt.

(Action: Children pretend to wash their face)

© Claire Walsh

Early years wishing well: Me and my home

Songs

Looking after ourselves

Personal, social and emotional development

★ Create very important routines for the children in your setting, such as washing their hands before they eat and after they have been to the toilet. Display bright cheerful notices that have painted handprints on them to remind the children of what they have to do every day.

★ Set up a doll and teddy bear hospital in the home corner. Invite the children to take on the roles of doctors and nurses diagnosing the patient's conditions and prescribing medicine.

Communication, language and literacy

★ Divide a piece of paper into four squares and encourage the children to draw four things that they must do to look after themselves. Cut out all their pictures and stick them into a scrapbook. With you acting as a scribe, ask the children to tell you what you should write on each page, such as 'You must comb your hair so that it looks tidy' and 'You must brush your teeth to keep them healthy'.

Mathematical development

★ Ask the children to count how many times we sing 'brush' in the song. Can they clap the number out? How many times do we sing 'carefully' in the song? Can they clap the number out?

Knowledge and understanding of the world

★ Show the children a variety of brushes such as a dustpan brush, a hairbrush, a dog brush, a toothbrush and a paintbrush. Help the children to name the brushes and decide what each brush should be used for and which ones they should use to look after themselves.

★ Encourage the children to think about where a germ might live in their house. Talk to them about why we have to keep particular rooms in our house really clean, such as the bathroom and the kitchen.

Physical development

★ Encourage the children to run their hand down their chest bone and then feel the pulsation of their heart beating. Carry out a short exercise routine to music and then get the children to feel their heart beat again. Ask them how they feel after they exercise and talk about why we should exercise regularly.

Creative development

★ Give each child a copy of the photocopiable sheet on page 93 and ask them to create their own toothbrush designs. Cut the toothbrushes out and display them.

★ Talk to the children about what a germ is. Help them to create their own germ monster using collage materials and strips of card, folded concertina fashion, for arms and legs. Ask them to think of a name for their germ and help them write it down on its 'body'.

Early years wishing well: Me and my home

Paint my face

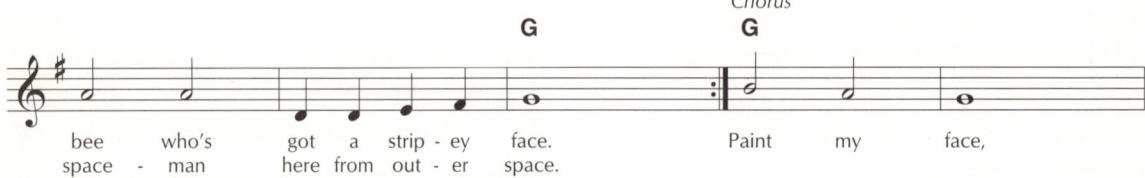

1. I could be a tiger living in the jungle. I could be a bee who's got a stripey face.

Chorus
Paint my face, make me something different. Paint my face, Make me something new.

2. I could be a clown who's funny in a circus. I could be a spaceman here from outer space.

2. I could be a monkey swinging in the treetops
I could be a rabbit running through a field.
I could be a panda if I really want to
I could be a cat if that is how I feel.

Paint my face
Make me something different.
Paint my face
Make me something new.

© Clive and Hannah Barnwell

Early years wishing well: Me and my home

Songs

Paint my face

Personal, social and emotional development
★ Have a fun day when you paint the children's faces with face paint. Check with parents that none of the children have sensitive skin and are allergic to face paint.
★ Why do the different animals in the song live in different places? What things do the animals need to live?

Communication, language and literacy
★ Encourage the children to draw a big picture of their face and label the parts using sounds. For example, they would write the letter 'e' for eyes and the letter 'n' for nose.
★ Ask the children to help you make a list of the animals mentioned in the song. Have they ever seen these animals? Can they describe what they look like? Go around the group inviting the children to tell you what each animal looks like, or what sounds it makes.

Mathematical development
★ Make some books for the children with five pages and a front and back cover. Show the children how to make their books by writing 'My number book' on the front cover, the number 1 and drawing one animal, such as a panda, on the first page, the number 2 and two monkeys on the second, and so on up to number 5. For younger children, draw the numbers in their books using a yellow felt-tipped pen and ask them to trace over them.

Knowledge and understanding of the world
★ Help the children to draw a picture of each of the animals listed in the song, in their own homes. Talk about how the home of a bee is different to the home of a rabbit.
★ Find out about some of the environments mentioned in the song. Can the children find out some facts about the jungle? What does it feel like there; is it hot or cold? Which animals live there?

Physical development
★ Shout out an animal's name such as a monkey and ask the children to walk like it.

Creative development
★ Encourage the children to paint a picture of their face and then display all the pictures in your room with a big sign saying 'Look at all our faces'.
★ Provide the children with paper plates and sticks and help them to paint the face of an animal mentioned in the song on it. Once the plate is dry, attach sticks and card to make ears. When the children sing the song, they can use their masks to help them really get into performing.
★ Help the children to make their own buzzing bee by sewing two circular pieces of yellow felt together and stuffing it. Sew on a strip of black felt and two pieces of net for wings. Sew on a piece of elastic and show the children how to hang their bees up.

71

Early years wishing well: Me and my home

Which face today?

Thoughtfully
Capo 3rd fret

Your face says a lot about the way you feel inside, Hungry, angry or bursting with pride.

Sleep-y, weep-y, perhaps you've lost your way, So what sort of face will you wear to-day?

© Sue Nicholls

Songs

Which face today?

Personal, social and emotional development

★ During circle time, pass a smile around the group. Start it off by smiling at the child next to you, who then smiles at the person next to them, until the smile has been passed all the way around the circle. Do the same with an angry face and a sad face.

★ Ask the children to think of someone who they can talk to when their feelings are hurt, such as their parents, their friends or a pet.

Communication, language and literacy

★ With the children, make a list of all the feelings in the song and draw the right expression that someone would have, if they were having that feeling, next to the word so that all the children understand. Ask the children to think of other feelings that they might know about.

Mathematical development

★ Show the children examples of three-dimensional shapes (food packaging is often a very good example) such as a cone, a triangular prism, a cube, a cylinder, a cuboid, a sphere, a pyramid and ask the children to count how many faces they can see.

★ Provide the children with a long strip of paper and a template of a circle. Show them how to draw around the circle along the strip. Then ask them to draw a happy face on the first circle, and a sad face on the second. Encourage them to continue with the repeating pattern that they have created.

Knowledge and understanding of the world

★ Ask the children to think about what else they know that has feelings. Hopefully, someone will suggest that animals do and that we should treat them with care and respect. You could contact the RSPCA, Causeway, Horsham, West Sussex RH12 1HG, tel: 0870-4443127 for their information packs and posters about animal welfare.

Physical development

★ Shout out a feeling to the children and ask them to travel around the room with the feeling. For example, if you shout 'happy', they may skip; if you shout 'tired', they may walk slowly, stretching and yawning and then curling up into a tiny little ball.

Creative development

★ Go through the words of the song with the children and talk to them about how the sound of our voices reflects how we feel. For example, ask them how we could say 'angry' and how we could say 'sad'.

★ Encourage the children to draw a picture of their face expressing a feeling. Provide them with mirrors so that they really know what they look like when they try to communicate a feeling. Make a book of all the children's feelings and call it 'We all have feelings'.

Songs

A pet to call my own

(Tune: 'Mary Had a Little Lamb')

1. I would like a little dog, Bow wow wow! Bow wow wow!
I would like a little dog, A pet to call my own.

2. I would like a little cat,
Miaow miaow miaow!
Miaow miaow miaow!
I would like a little cat,
A pet to call my own.

3. I would like a little bird,
Tweet tweet tweet!
Tweet tweet tweet!
I would like a little bird,
A pet to call my own.

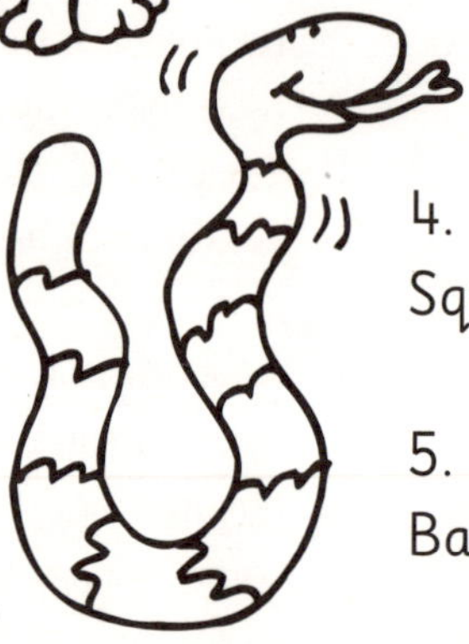

4. I would like a little mouse,
Squeak squeak squeak...

5. I would like a little lamb
Baa baa baa...

6. I would like a little snake
Hiss hiss hiss

How many animals can you think of?

© Johanne Levy

Early years wishing well: Me and my home

Songs

A pet to call my own

Personal, social and emotional development

★ Ask the children to name a pet that they would like to own and to give a reason why.
★ Encourage the children to bring in a photograph of their pets to talk about where they sleep and what they like to do. Those children who do not have a pet could bring in a picture of an animal cut from a newspaper or magazine.

Communication, language and literacy

★ Draw an outline of a cat on your board and ask the children to think of words that they know to describe a cat. Write the children's words inside the cat outline and display in your room. Repeat this activity with other animals that are in the song, such as a bird, a mouse or a lamb.
★ During circle time, go around and ask the children to say words that rhyme with cat such as fat, mat and rat.

Mathematical development

★ Copy the photocopiable sheet on page 94 onto card. Cut up the cards as shown and give a set to each child. Show the children how to count the cats' legs. Ask them questions such as, 'If one cat has four legs, how many legs do two cats have together?'. Encourage them to draw pictures of animals and to ask their friends to count how many legs they can see.

Knowledge and understanding of the world

★ Give the children some pictures of animals and ask them to place them in certain areas in your setting such as the sand tray, dolls' house and garage. Could a cat live in the sand tray or would it be happier in the dolls' house? Would a camel be happier in the sand tray or in the garage?
★ Provide the children with a variety of cards that have animal footprints on them. Then give them a second set of cards representing animal homes. Encourage them to match the home card with the animal card.

Physical development

★ Sit the children in a circle and choose a child to start the activity. Ask them to walk around the circle and place their hand on each child's head saying 'duck'. When they get to the child they want to be chased by, they shout 'goose'. That child then jumps up and chases the lead child around the circle back to the place that they have just left.
★ Practise moving like the different animals mentioned in the song. Can the children scurry like a mouse or slither like a snake?

Creative development

★ Provide the children with clay and Plasticine and encourage them to make a pet. Give them a variety of tools that they can use to shape the clay and encourage them to add features to make faces on their pets.

Early years wishing well: Me and my home

Celebration!

(Tune: 'Humpty Dumpty')

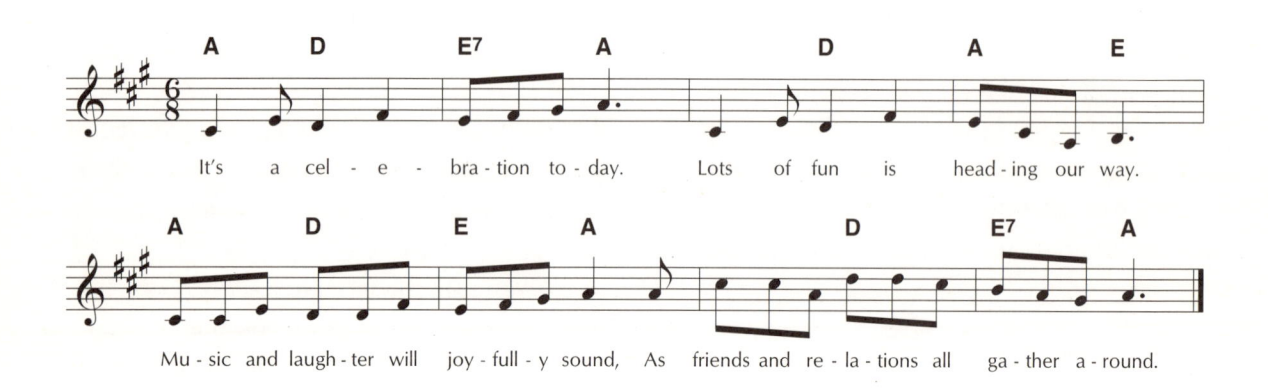

It's a cel-e-bra-tion to-day. Lots of fun is head-ing our way.
Mu-sic and laugh-ter will joy-ful-ly sound, As friends and re-la-tions all ga-ther a-round.

This song can be used for any celebration, and it can also be adapted for a birthday party by substituting the words, 'It's a birthday party today' in place of the first line.

Alternatively, here is another verse written specifically for a birthday party:

Come and share my birthday today.
Please come round and then we can play.
We'll pass the parcel and then we'll have tea.
Oh what a lovely day it will be!

© Johanne Levy

Songs

Celebration!

Personal, social and emotional development

★ Have a discussion about what a celebration is and what feelings we have when we celebrate. Discuss where we have celebrations and how they do not always have to be in our own home.

★ Ask each child to bring in a photograph from home of their most recent celebration (Christmas, or their birthday) and to talk about it to the rest of the children.

Communication, language and literacy

★ Tell the children that you want to organize a monsters' tea party and that you want them to help you. Make a list on your board of all the jobs that need to be done when we have a real celebration, such as making a shopping list, making a guest list, writing and sending invitations.

★ Help the children to write invitations to a soft toy of their choice, preferably a monster! Ensure that the children know the type of information that should be included such as the day, time and location of the party.

★ Invite the children to make name cards that can be laid out on the party table.

Mathematical development

★ As you give out the party food, point out to the children how important it is to share out food equally and fairly. Show them how to cut a cake in half and then into quarters.

★ Practise laying a table for a party in the home corner. Encourage the children to set places for four people, putting out four plates, cups and bowls.

Knowledge and understanding of the world

★ Help the children to make their own food to eat at the party such as bread rolls or jelly.

★ Ask the children to think about what different foods they have eaten at different celebrations. Have they been sweet or savoury? Encourage them to think about Christmas logs, Divali barfi, Easter biscuits and birthday cakes and to express their opinions about these special foods.

★ Invite parents to your setting to demonstrate how to make a variety of traditional celebration foods.

Physical development

★ A party needs games! Play musical statues, musical bumps, musical cushions, and finally, sleeping lions to calm everyone down.

Creative development

★ Help the children to make individual place mats by weaving strips of paper together. Seal the ends with clear sticky tape, not glue as the children will need to put food on them.

★ Make crowns, out of card or paper, to wear at the party. Invite the children to make a repeating pattern on their finished crowns using coloured pens.

Early years wishing well: Me and my home

Animal sounds

Alphabet washing line

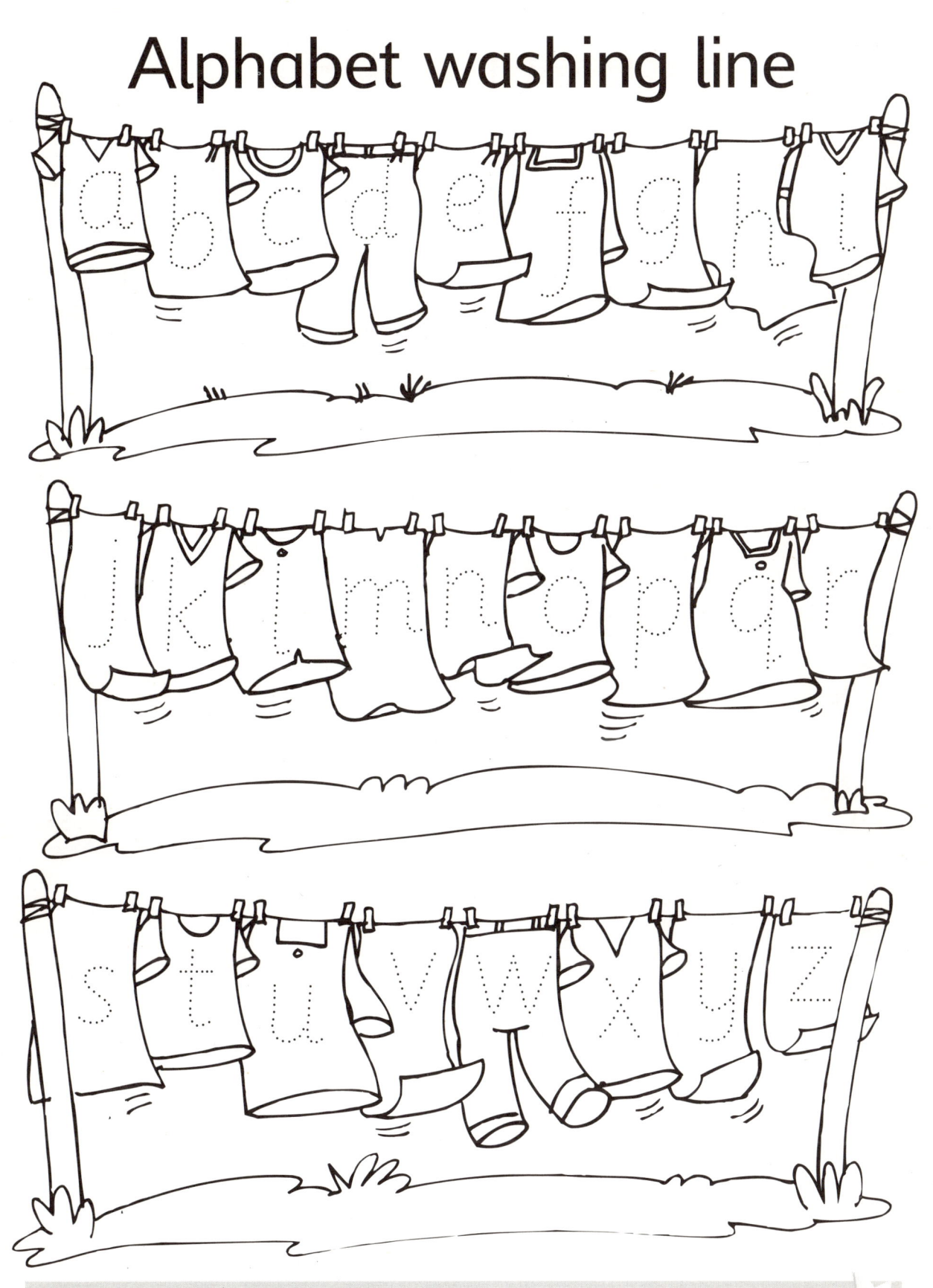

a b c d e f g h i

j k l m n o p q r

s t u v w x y z

Early years wishing well: Me and my home

Photocopiables

Colourful bear

green
green
green
red red
black black
black
yellow yellow
green
blue blue
red red

80 photocopiable — Early years wishing well: Me and my home

Food, glorious food

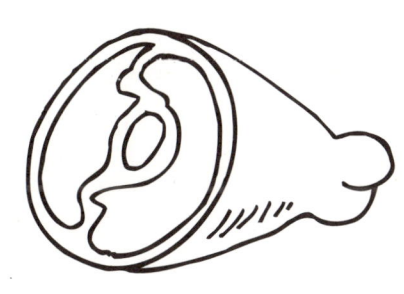

grapefruit	jam	pizza
ham	apples	cheese
pancakes	peas	ice-cream

Early years wishing well: Me and my home

Pussy cat, pussy cat

Lift-the-flap freezer

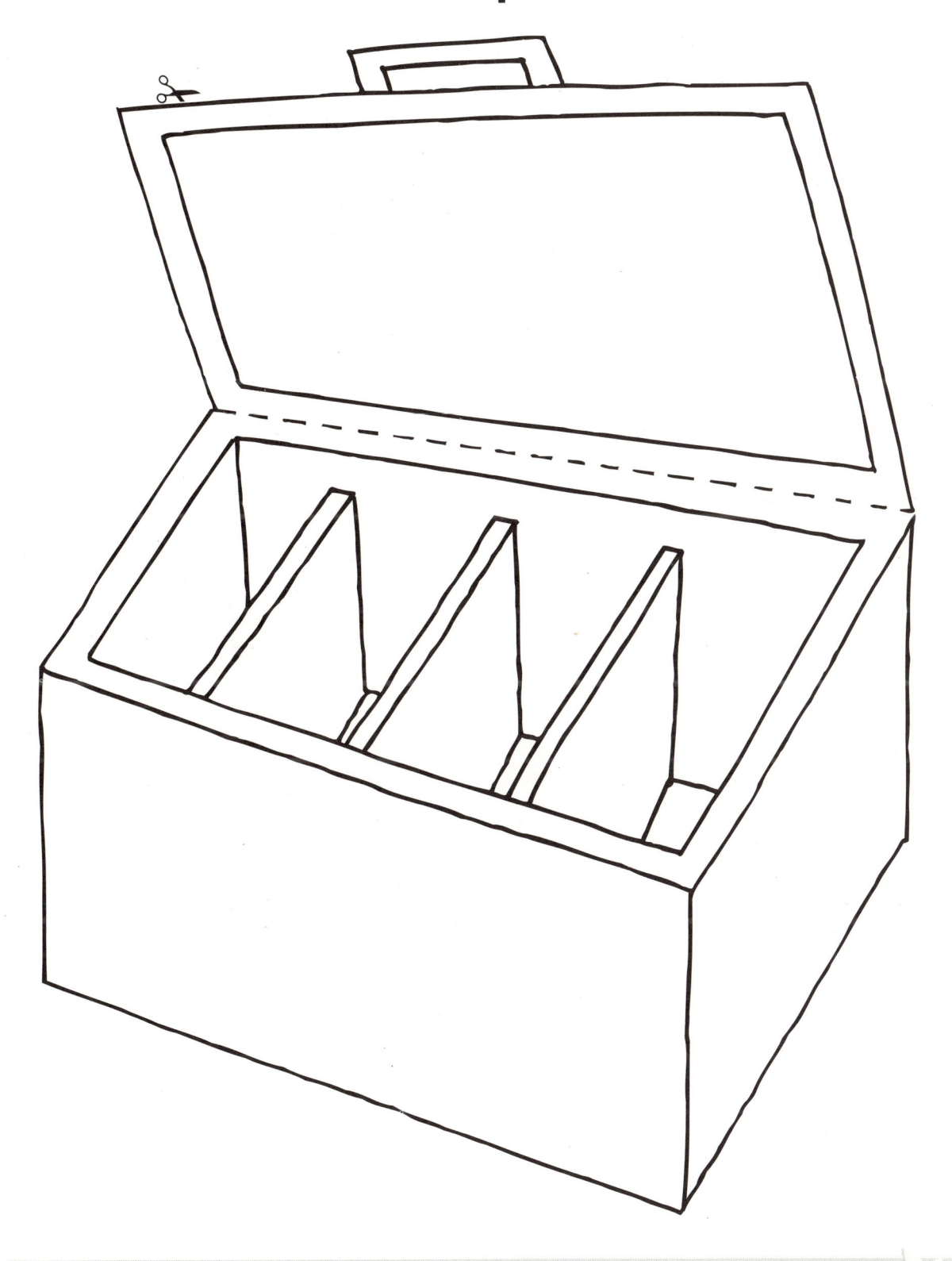

Early years wishing well: Me and my home

Word bingo dice

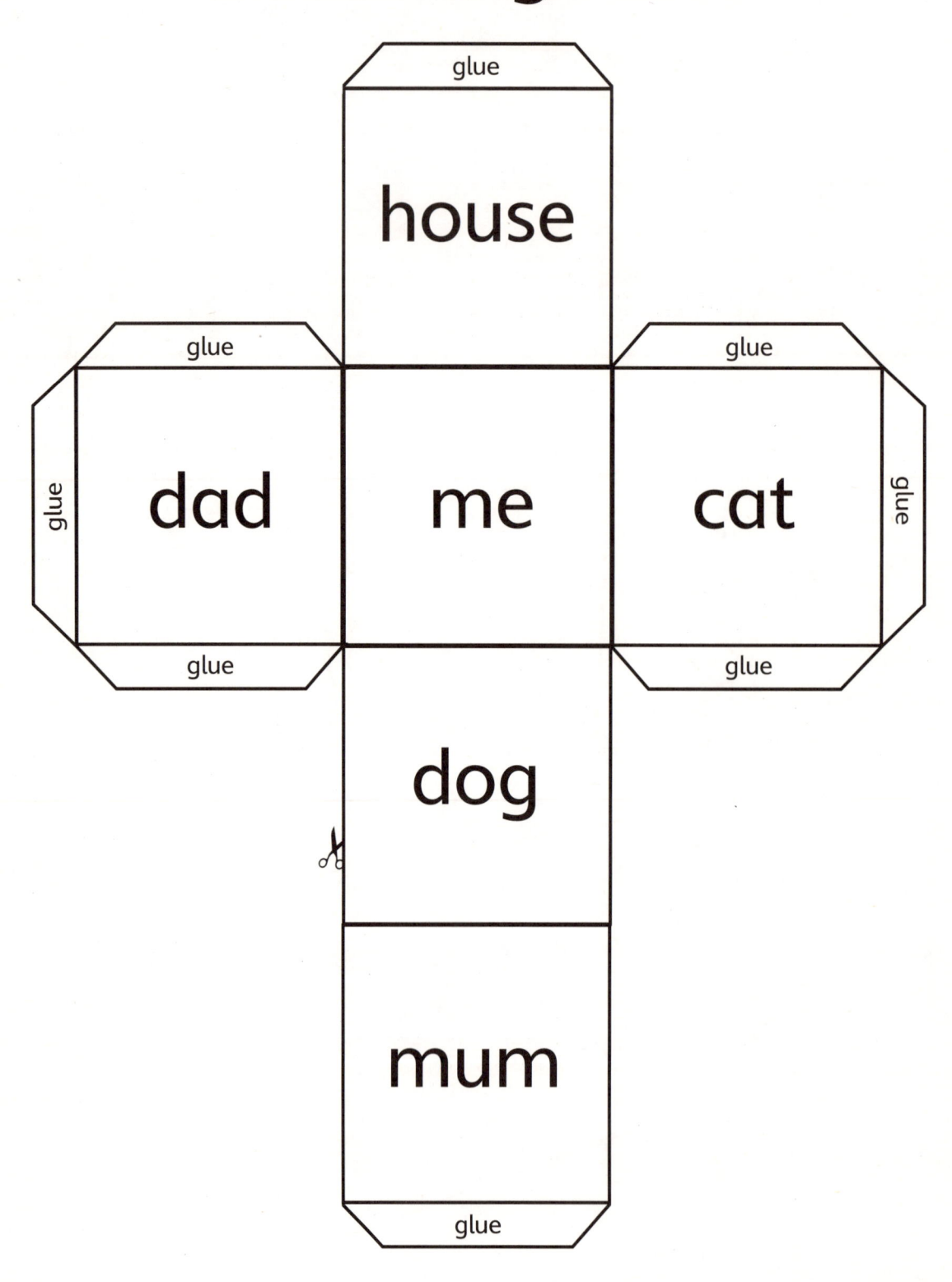

	glue	
	house	

glue		glue
dad	me	cat
glue		glue

dog

mum
glue

84 *photocopiable* — Early years wishing well: Me and my home

Word bingo board

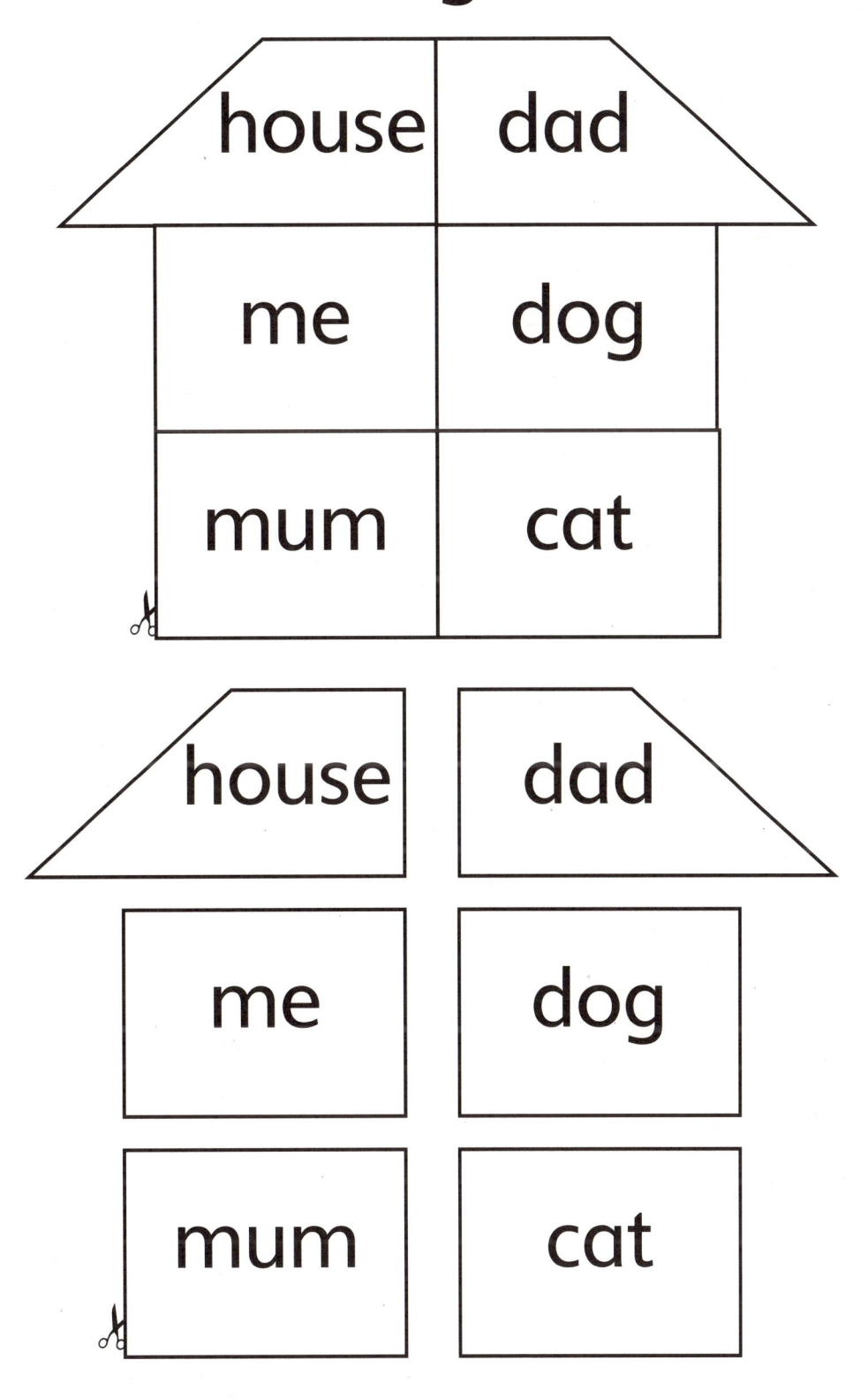

house	dad
me	dog
mum	cat

house	dad
me	dog
mum	cat

Early years wishing well: Me and my home

Shape pictures

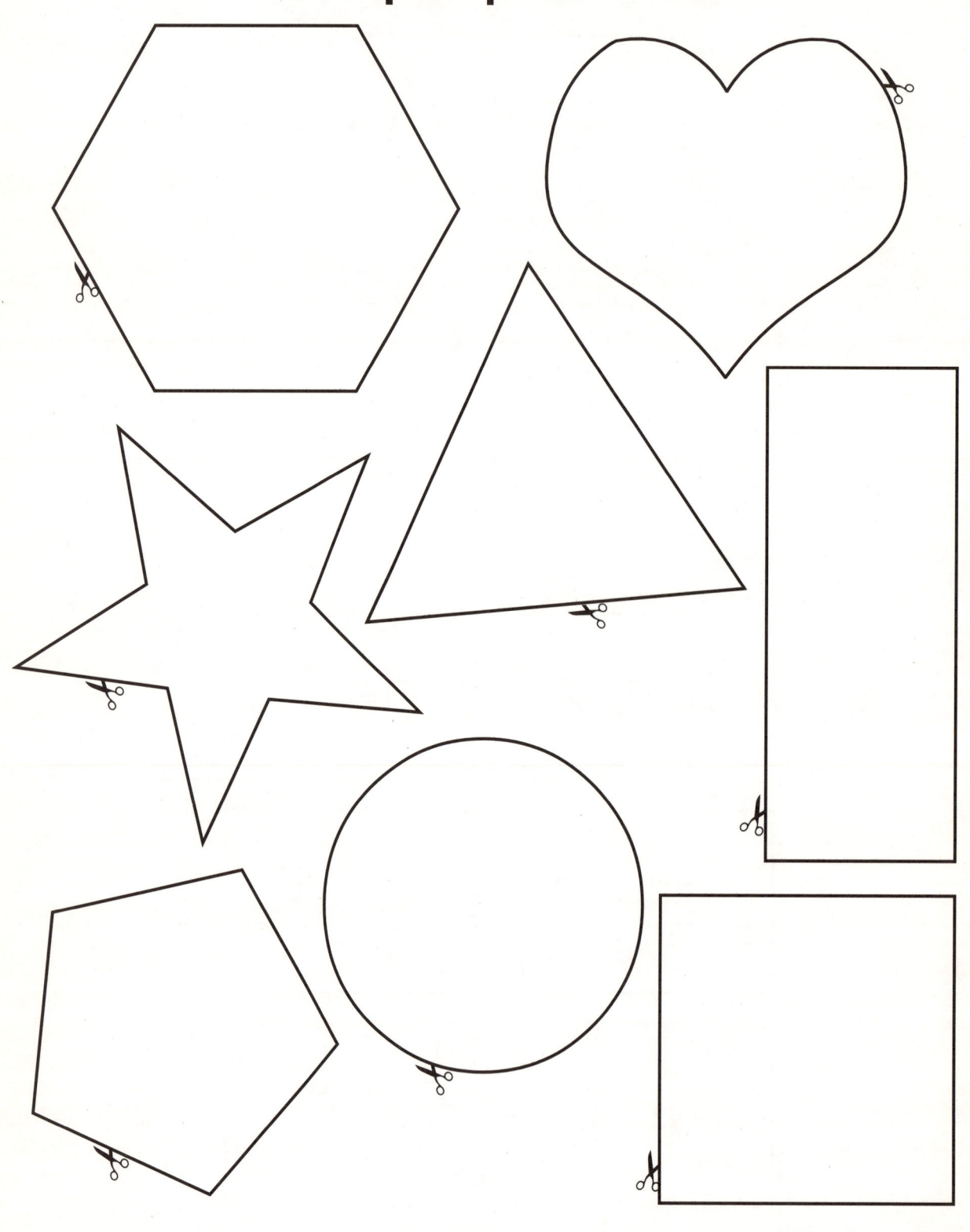

86 *photocopiable* — Early years wishing well: Me and my home

Puppet show

Early years wishing well: Me and my home

Patterned tie

Blast off!

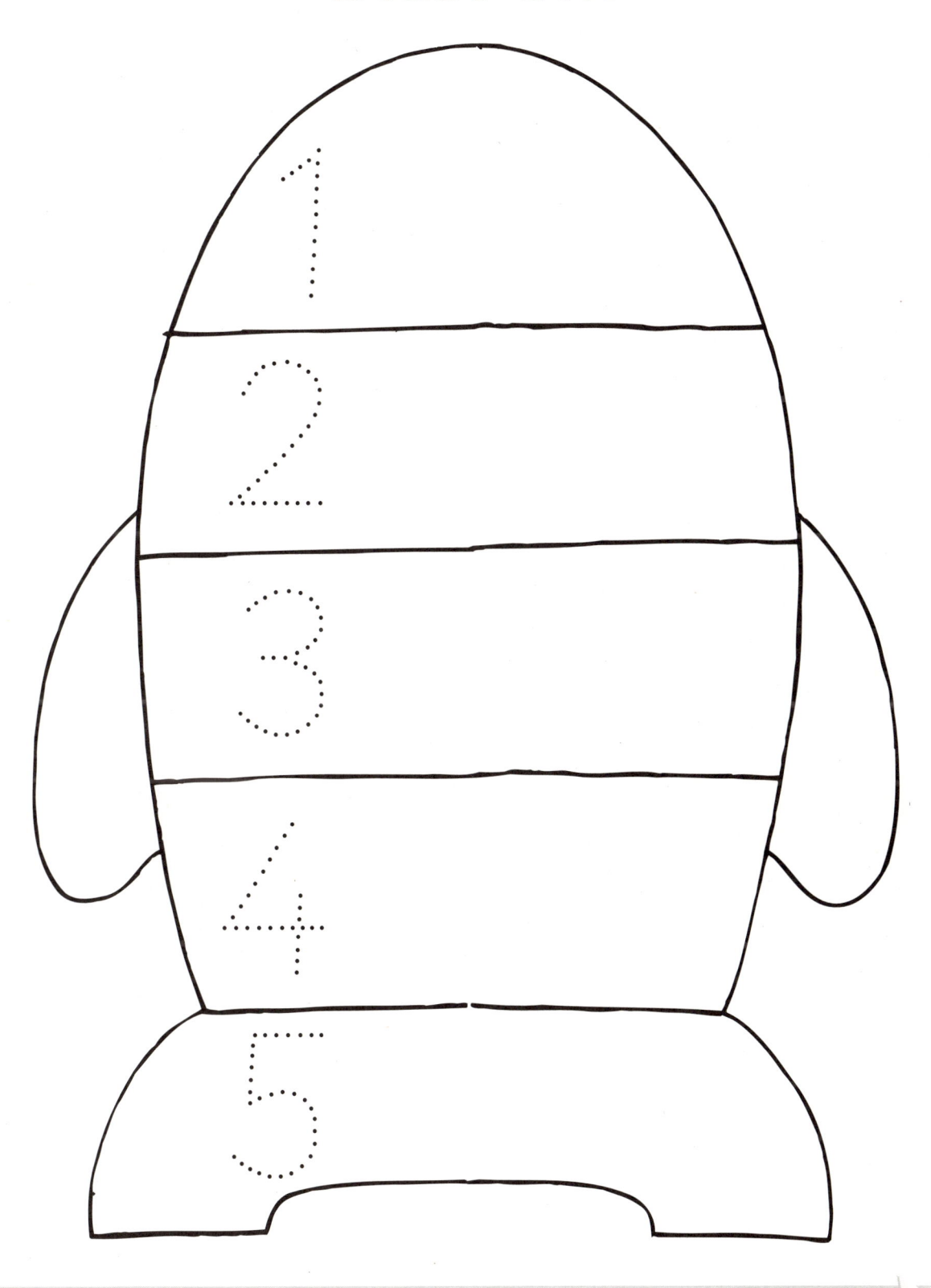

Early years wishing well: Me and my home

Photocopiables

My special day

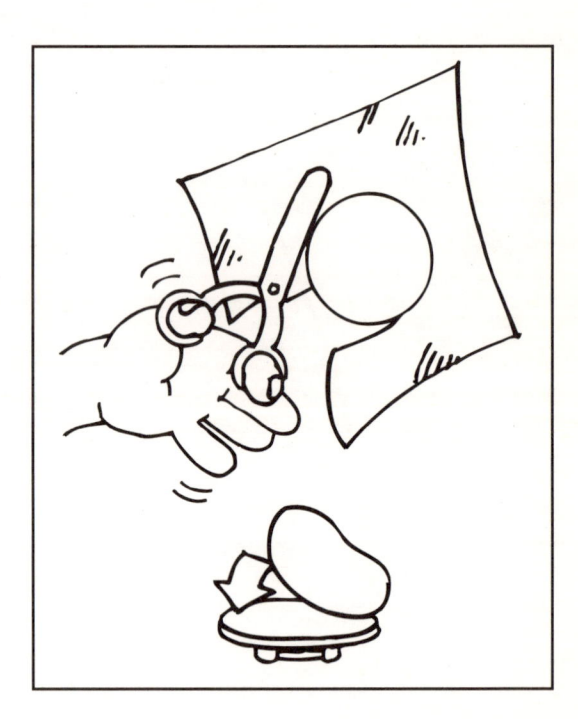

I'm special

Dear ....

Tomorrow is your special day. It would be really nice if you could bring in your favourite teddy bear, book and perhaps some photographs of yourself and your family.

Love from

....

Glasses and flowers

Early years wishing well: Me and my home

Flower power

Photocopiables

Toothbrush design

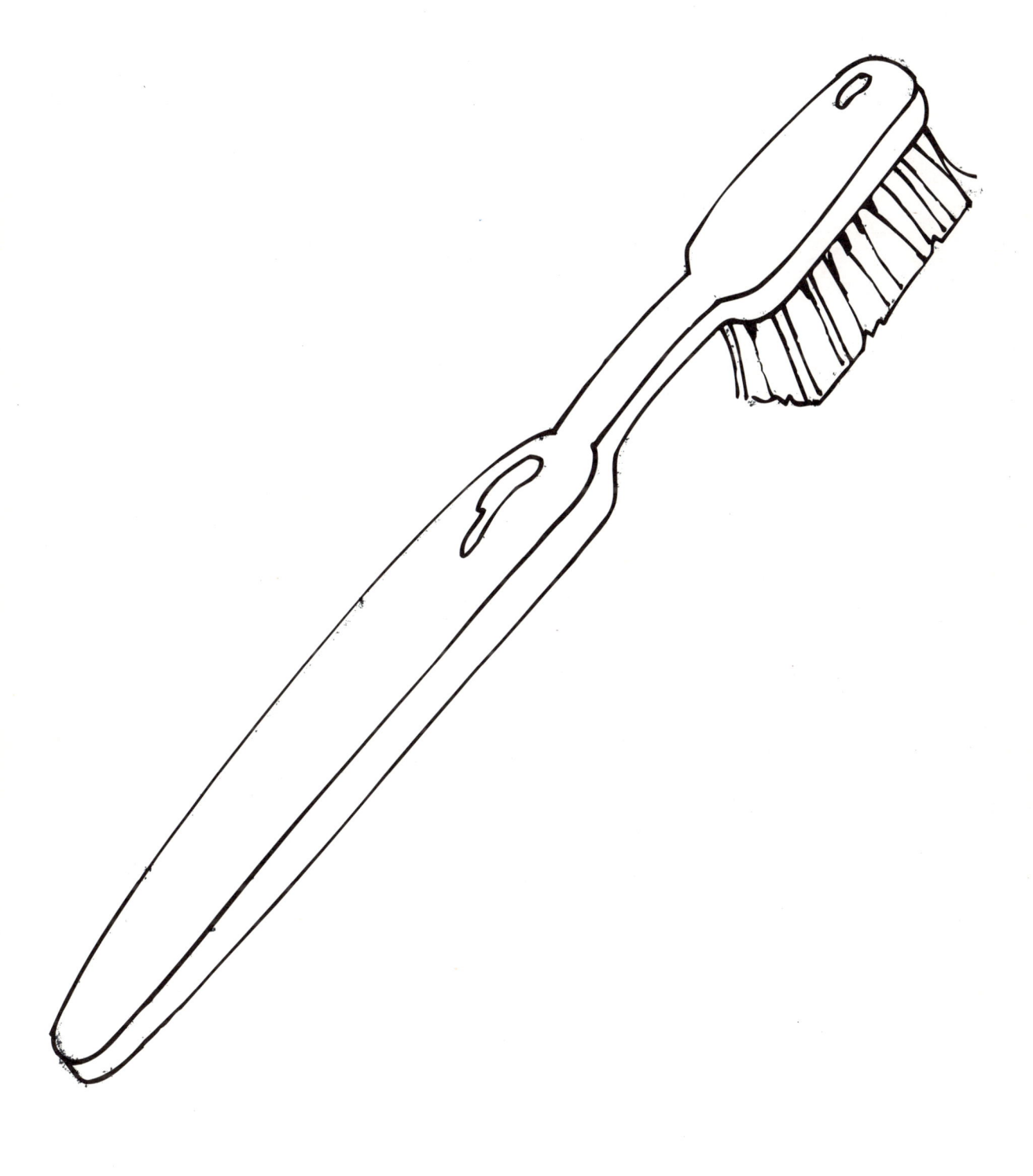

Early years wishing well: Me and my home — photocopiable 93

Cats' legs

Dot to dot

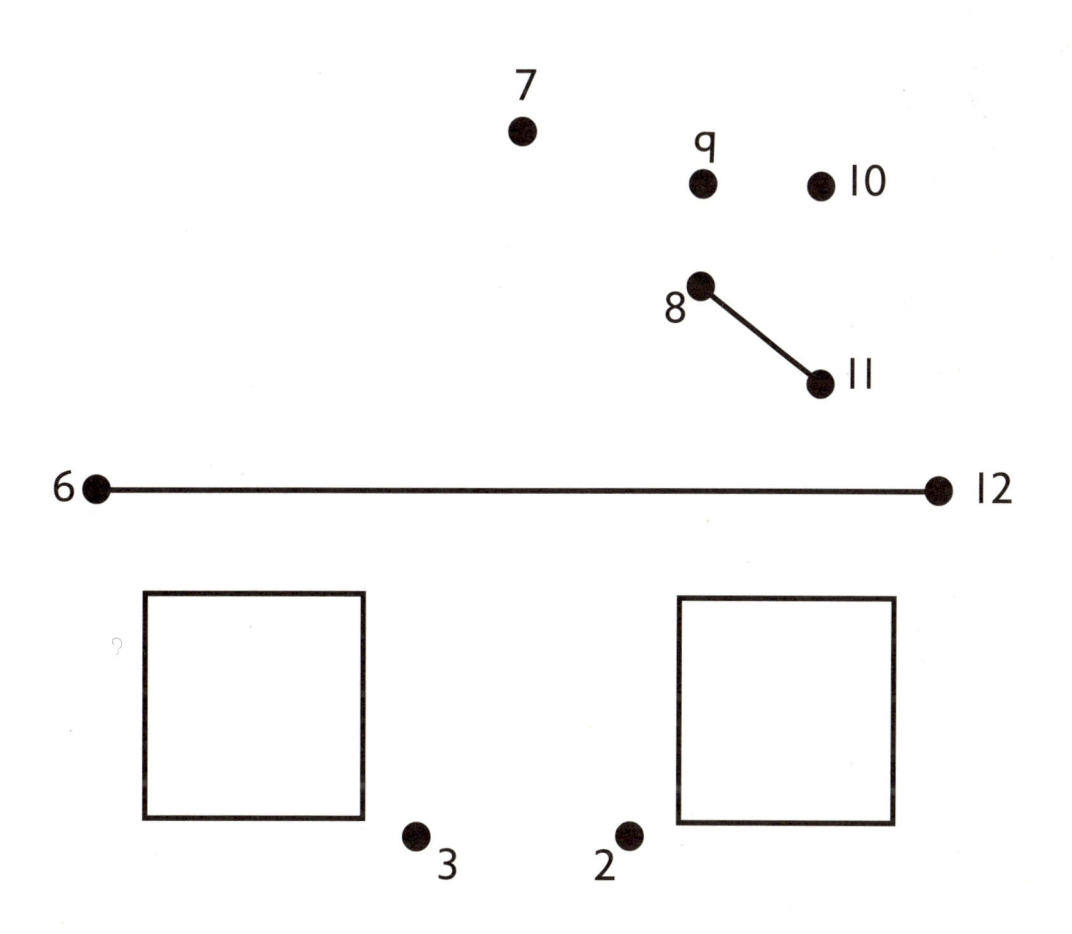

Early years wishing well: Me and my home

Photocopiables

The flap house

★ Photocopy onto paper and cut out.

★ Cut along the lines to make the door and windows.

★ Stick onto card and decorate the house. Draw some people inside.

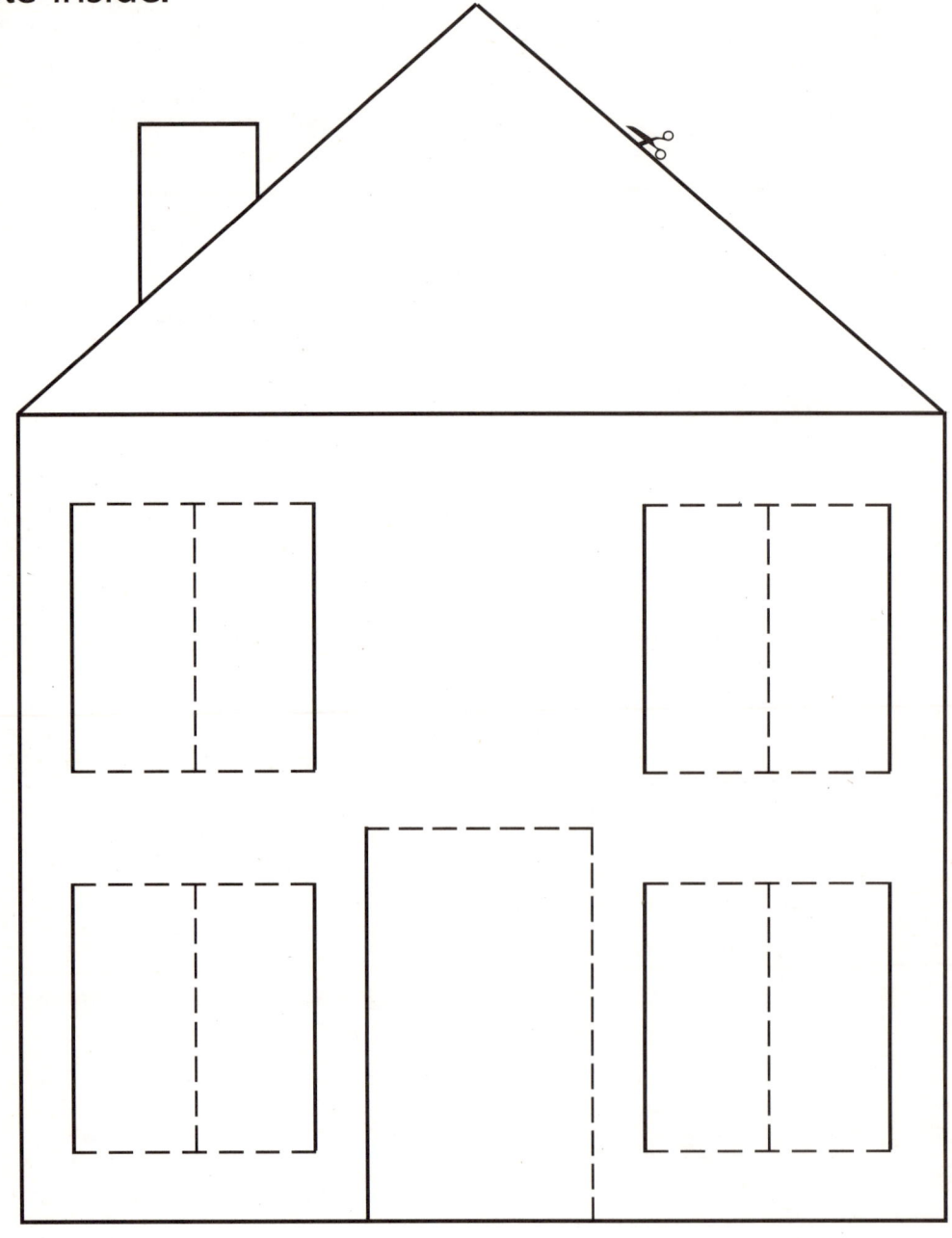

96 *photocopiable* Early years wishing well: Me and my home